D0378422

Who Will Be Saved?

Now is the day of salvation.
—*2 Corinthians 6:2*

Who Will Be Saved?

WILLIAM H. WILLIMON

Abingdon Press
Nashville

WHO WILL BE SAVED?

Copyright © 2008 by Abingdon Press

All rights reserved.

No part of this work may be reproduced or transmitted in any form or by any means, electronic or mechanical, including photocopying and recording, or by any information storage or retrieval system, except as may be expressly permitted by the 1976 Copyright Act or in writing from the publisher. Requests for permission should be addressed to Abingdon Press, P.O. Box 801, 201 Eighth Avenue South, Nashville, TN 37202-0801, or e-mailed to permissions@abingdonpress.com.

This book is printed on acid-free paper.

Library of Congress Cataloging-in-Publication Data

Willimon, William H.
    Who will be saved? / William H. Willimon.
        p. cm.
    Includes bibliographical references and index.
    ISBN 978-0-687-65119-1 (binding: adhesive perfect : alk. paper)
    1. Salvation--Christianity.   I. Title.

    BT751.3.W54 2008
    234—dc22

                                                                    2007051117

All scripture quotations unless noted otherwise are taken from the New Revised Standard Version of the Bible, copyright 1989, Division of Christian Education of the National Council of the Churches of Christ in the United States of America. Used by permission. All rights reserved.

Scripture noted as KJV is taken from the King James or Authorized Version of the Bible.

Scripture noted as NIV is taken from the Holy Bible, NEW INTERNATIONAL VERSION®. Copyright © 1973, 1978, 1984 by International Bible Society. All rights reserved throughout the world. Used by permission of International Bible Society.

08 09 10 11 12 13 14 15 16 17—10 9 8 7 6 5 4 3 2 1
MANUFACTURED IN THE UNITED STATES OF AMERICA

For
William Henry and Parker Thomas

CONTENTS

Preface ix

One: The God Who Refuses to Be Alone 1

Two: The Eros of God 21

Three: Divine Abundance 35

Four: Christ Triumphant 53

Five: Damned? 69

Six: What About Them? 93

Seven: Strange Salvation 109

A Concluding Postscript 135

Notes 137

Scripture Index 143

Index of Names 149

PREFACE

Interviewed in 1966, singer Bob Dylan reported that he had "done everything I wanted to do." If that were the case, to what had Dylan to look forward? Dylan deadpanned, "Salvation. Just plain salvation."[1]

I'm not sure if Dylan meant *salvation* as Christians use the word. When the interviewer pressed him Dylan added, "I'd also like to start a cookbook magazine. . . . I want to referee a heavyweight championship fight."[2] Although I have no reason to believe that Bob Dylan will ever read this book, I believe that clarification about salvation is in order.

How do Christians answer when asked, "Are you saved?" When we affirm in the Nicene Creed that Jesus came "for us and for our salvation," how is the word *salvation* properly used when related to Jesus Christ? Stanley Hauerwas says that the best preparation to be a pastor these days is to have previously been a teacher of high school French. The same skills that are required to pound French verbs into the heads of unwilling sixteen-year-olds are essential to training in the Christian faith. To be a Christian is to have growing proficiency in language called the gospel of Jesus Christ. Take this as an extended sermon on how to use salvation in a manner that is peculiarly Christian. Before I'm done, I'll also suggest how we are meant to practice salvation in all that we do. This is soteriology (*soter*, "to save") for everyone.

In my first days as chaplain at Duke University, a delegation of campus ministers asked my support for a "Declaration of Religious Rights and Freedoms on Campus." Their pronouncement assured Duke students that they would be "safe from unwanted evangelization." I reassured the group that it was unnecessary for me to sign such a declaration for they had nothing to fear from me: I was a Methodist. It had been so long since we had evangelized anybody on campus, wanted or not, that we had forgotten how.

When they resisted my self-characterization, I asked, "Name one Jew" (the campus rabbi was part of the group) "who has been evangelized by some Christian on our campus." They could not. As I saw it, interfaith marriage was the rabbi's big challenge, not interfaith "unwanted evangelization."

"Sadly," I said, "you are losing Jews to the same 'faith' to which many Christians succumb—unbridled, consumptive capitalism that renders a

Duke education into training to be more savvy consumers. Jews, Catholics, Protestants—anyone for whom 'success' is more than a big house and a big car—should be forewarned that when you send your kid to a first-rate, selective university like ours, she will come out less faithful than she went in."

It isn't that Christians are keen on salvation whereas others are not. It isn't that most people are too modern, too enlightened, and too sophisticated and secular to worry about something outmoded like salvation. It is rather that we live in a conflicted supermarket of salvations that are based on very different ideas of what or who saves. About the time that Jesus was born, an inscription was placed throughout the Roman colonies proclaiming the *euangelion* ("gospel") to the captive peoples that "Augustus has been sent to us as savior." So even though we say what salvation in Jesus Christ is, we shall also need to say what it is not. And in the church family of which I am a part, that takes some courage. Our now dominant faith is that though there are different faiths, they are all fairly much the same. This is the sort of thing that people say when they are unwilling to admit that different faiths (and their different salvations) may actually be *different.*

To say that Christian salvation is a peculiar, distinctive, even odd way of life and death is to threaten the dominant status quo that believes that differences in belief are dangerous, a threat to national unity. Religious differences must therefore be suppressed or trivialized in order to keep us religious fanatics from killing one another. This essay on Christian salvation takes another way in its unabashed, even joyful celebration of the Christian difference that is salvation in Jesus Christ. As Paul said of the plurality of salvations in his day, "Jews demand signs and Greeks desire wisdom, but we proclaim Christ crucified" (1 Cor 1:22-23).

Arguments over salvation are not only unhelpful but also tend to betray the subject. Arguments imply that if we could just get our heads straight about salvation, we would be in tight with God. I believe that salvation is not what we think but what God in Christ thinks, so this book will not be much of an argument. This book is testimony, an attempt to give a short "accounting for the hope that is [within us]" (1 Pet 3:15). Having met salvation in Jesus Christ, Christians tend to spend the rest of our lives singing about, getting ready for, attempting to obey the implications of that salvation, and testifying to anybody who will listen. Salvation is when we receive the big picture, when we are let in on the secret of what's going on in the world since Immanuel, when God grants a present glimpse of that which God will one day show us in glorious intensity—when Christ shall be not only over all but also in all, for all, and with all. *Salvation* is a word that Christian theologians use for the Christian life as a whole, for reality in the peculiar, definitive light of Jesus Christ.

Do you want a good working definition of *salvation*? *Jesus Christ* in all that he is and all that he does.

At the end of the Letter to the Ephesians, Paul tells early Christians to vest with various sorts of armament to withstand the wiles of the devil—the sword of the Spirit, the shield of faith, the breastplate of righteousness. He finally urges them to put on "the helmet of salvation" (Eph 6:17). Salvation is here depicted is a sort of defensive armor, a helmet that protects Christians from losing consciousness, from being bopped on the brain by the world and forgetting who they are. I'd be happy if this book helps in that defensive endeavor.

Thanks to Jason Byassee, Drew Clayton, Wade Langer, Denise Morgan Mullaney, Kip Laxon, Tim Whitaker, Brooks Lumpkin, and other colleagues who reacted to this book in process. Thanks to President Ted Wardlaw and the Austin Presbyterian Theological Seminary faculty for their hospitality during the Thomas White Currie Lectureship. Once again, thanks to Keith and Brenda Brodie and the Devonwood Foundation for their generous support for research.

William H. Willimon
Bishop
Birmingham, Alabama
The First Sunday in Lent

CHAPTER ONE

THE GOD WHO REFUSES
TO BE ALONE

When thoughts of a book on salvation were percolating in me, a friend of some years approached me with a question that had become his obsession. He told me that he grew up in a small-town Baptist church. As a youth he "accepted Jesus as [his] personal savior and [he] knew that [he] was saved." He was active in church until his late teenaged years when other interests drew him away. As a young man, when he married, he returned to the church, partly because of his wife's piety.

Now, in midlife he had become obsessed with the question, "Am I really saved?" He had begun to doubt that he had ever had a true conversion experience. He had engaged in a study of the Bible, but that had filled him with more questions. He had tried to discuss his plight with a number of pastors and friends, but they all seemed to have different points of view that confused him all the more. He used to pray, but had stopped because it felt like he was just "talking to [him]self."

"What if I died tomorrow?" he asked. "I'm not sure that I would be saved and go to heaven."

I told my friend that God had sent him to me to reassure me that we needed another book on salvation!

My heart went out to this brother who was in real torment and consternation. I could make a number of observations about his struggle with salvation, but for now I'll just note the absence of one key player: God. My friend characterized his struggle as his lonely battle to understand, his solitary attempt to decide, his need to feel, and his heroic efforts to be certain. I asked my friend to consider the possibility that his turmoil might be God induced, that God might be using this turbulence to move him to some new plane in their relationship. Perhaps his struggle was validation that God was indeed real and that God was working to draw him closer. Perhaps.

The modern world teaches us to narrate our lives without reference to God. It's all our decisions, our actions, our feelings, and our desires. So the first thing we must say is that *salvation is primarily about God.*

How does it stand between us and God? In Scripture the question is never, "Is there a God?" but rather, "Does the God who is there care about us?" W. H. Auden depicts the modern task of learning to live in a universe now emptied of concern for humanity:

> Looking up at the stars, I know quite well
> That, for all they care, I can go to hell.[1]

Auden goes on to assure us that the universe's failure to take notice need cause us little concern. If anything, we should be concerned about the attention we draw to ourselves here on earth, be it admiration or admonishment. But no matter who observes us on earth or from heaven, Auden suggests that we can get used to anything. Given opportunity, we could decide even a sky emptied of its stars is a beautiful and fitting thing.

With time we adjust to cosmic indifference. A favorite means of coping with the absence of a savior is to deny that we need saving. One of my cherished viewpoints of the National Cathedral in Washington DC is the sculptured tympanum over the front door. Medieval interpreters spoke of the tympanum as a component of the "doorway of heaven," the "gateway to God," because it was here that one entered the cathedral and also the glories of the Christian faith.

In almost every medieval cathedral that space is occupied by a depiction of the Last Judgment. One thinks of Notre Dame de Paris where a judging angel holds scales, weighing the merits of the good and the bad. Over Notre Dame's scene of judgment, blessedness, and damnation presides the enthroned Christ, surrounded by his faithful apostles. In some churches Mary, mother of Jesus, is on the tympanum, and sometimes Christ is on the cross.

At the National Cathedral the contemporary sculptor Frederick Hart has rendered a peculiarly twentieth-century biblical subject—the creation of humanity. It's a Rodin-like, sensuous Adam and Eve emerging from the hand of a creative God. Gone is any sense of the judging, saving God. God's greatest work is no longer the cross or our redemption; the greatest divine work is our creation. Neither atonement nor reconciliation but rather creation of humanity has become the message that the church celebrates before the world.

This suggests humanity overly impressed with itself, getting along just fine, thank you. Our great desire is to be successful in achieving the human project, as we define it, immune from the judgments of God, rather than to be redeemed through the judgments of God. To paraphrase dear Flannery O'Connor, anybody with reasonable success in being successful, or even a good car, "don't need redemption."

No enthroned or even crucified cosmic Christ to be seen because, well, if you are as knowledgeable, as grand and glorious as contemporary North Americans, there is not much left for God to do for us. God gave us a grand start in fashioning us from the dirt at Creation, then retired, leaving us to fend for our gifted selves.

(By the way, at Duke Chapel, where I preached for twenty years, the tympanum is occupied by none other than John Wesley! So who am I to criticize the National Cathedral's tympanum?)

Although celebration of humanity is the dominant, governmentally sanctioned story, it is not the story to which Christians are accountable. It is the conventional North American story that, at every turn, is counter to the gospel. Thus we begin by noting that there are few more challenging words to be said by the church than *salvation*. Salvation implies that there is something from which we need to be saved, that we are not doing as well as we presume, that we do not have the whole world in our hands and that the hope for us is not of our devising.

Most Christians think of salvation as related exclusively to the afterlife. Salvation is when we die and get to go to heaven. To be sure, Scripture is concerned with our eternal fate. What has been obscured is Scripture's stress on salvation as invitation to share in a particular God's life here, now, so that we might do so forever. Salvation isn't just a destination; it is our vocation. Salvation isn't just a question of who is saved and who is damned, who will get to heaven and how, but also how we are swept up into participation in the mystery of God who is Jesus Christ. Get a biblical concordance and check the references to heaven and you will find that almost none of them are related to "death." Heaven is when or where one is fully with God—salvation.

Look up *salvation* in the concordance and you will find a wide array of images. Luke-Acts uses the word *salvation* rather frequently, Matthew and Mark almost never, though we ought not to make too much of that. All of the Gospels may be fairly read as stores about the rich, peculiar nature of salvation in Jesus Christ. Salvation is a claim about God. God's self-assigned task is "working salvation in the earth" (Ps 74:12). God is addressed as "God of our salvation" (Ps 65:5). For some, salvation is rescue, deliverance, and victory. For others, it is healing, wholeness, completion, and rest. Isaiah speaks of salvation as a great economic reversal in which God gives a free banquet for the poor (Isaiah 55). Whatever salvation means, its meaning must be too rich for any single definition. [2]

SALVATION AS GOD'S WORK

"The salvation of this human world lies nowhere else than in the human heart, in the human power to reflect, in human meekness and human responsibility," declared Václav Havel.[3] Considering how Havel suffered at the hands of the Communists, it is touching for him still to think so highly of human prospects. Yet Havel's is a most conventional, limitedly modern thought—salvation is what we do by ourselves to save ourselves.

In Scripture, salvation is what God does. Despite my foregoing reservations about the implicit arrogance of the tympanum of the National Cathedral, salvation is creation, or re-creation. In Genesis, God does not really create the world out of nothing, *ex nihilo*, but rather works on the dark and formless void. Creation is that good that would not be there if God were not the sort of God who God is. God addresses the chaotic, formless stuff of darkness with, "Let there be light!" God speaks to the chaos, and in that address there is evocation of a world that God calls "good." Creation is depicted in Genesis as a series of divine addresses. There is something about this God that speaks something out of nothing by commanding, summoning, addressing, calling, and preaching. Salvation, seen from this perspective, is a primary product of divine love, the grand result after a creative God goes to work with words.

With Pharaoh's chariots pursuing them, the children of Israel falter on the bank of the Red Sea. Moses encourages them with, "Do not be afraid, stand firm, and see the deliverance that the LORD will accomplish for you today" (Exod 14:13). Upon arriving on the opposite shore, safe from the Egyptians, Moses leads Israel in a hymn, singing "the LORD is my strength and my might, and he has become my salvation" (Exod 15:2).

Theologian Karl Barth taught that salvation was the whole point of Creation.[4] God creates humanity a world so that God might have a grand stage on which to enact the drama of redemption. When the God who brought forth the world comes so very near to us in Jesus Christ, salvation is the name for that decisive encounter. John 1 implies that Incarnation is salvation, an intensification of what God has been doing since Genesis 1. "The Word became flesh and lived among us" (v. 14). When God goes to work, makes a move, comes close (Incarnation) that work (God in action) is salvation (God triumphant). As Charles Wesley put it in a Christmas hymn, Jesus Christ is God "contracted to a span, incomprehensibly made man." All of our lives are lived in the light of a prior choice—not our choice, but God's. Early on, even before we got here, God chose never to be God except as God with us, God for us in Christ Jesus.[5]

> And let the skies rain down righteousness;
> let the earth open, that salvation may spring up, . . .
> I the LORD have created it. (Isa 45:8)

Because most of what we know for sure about God is based upon what God does, it is possible to say that salvation is not only what God does but also who God is. Whoever would make a world for the sheer delight of relationship and conversation, whoever would work a miracle like raising crucified Jesus Christ from the dead is properly known as "The God who saves."

> Surely God is my salvation;
>   I will trust, and will not be afraid,
> for the LORD GOD is my strength and my might;
>   he has become my salvation. (Isa 12:2)

We would never know who God is if it were not for our having seen, touched, and tasted God's salvation in Jesus Christ (1 John 1:1). Though we could not come to God, God came to us in a stunning and peculiar act of salvation, and thereby showed us as much of God as we need to know.

The Hebrew verb root *ya sha* ("save") is found 354 times in the Old Testament, usually with God as subject. Proper names derived from this root—Elisha, Joshua, and Hosea—indicate "God saves." Later, Matthew will underscore the theological significance of Jesus' name (Hebrew "Joshua") with a commentary by the angel, "he will save his people from their sins" (Matt 1:21). When Jesus is welcomed into Jerusalem, people will shout "Hosanna!" (Mark 11:9), "Save us we pray," from the Hebrew *hosi anna.*

I find it remarkable that *salvation* appears most frequently in Psalms and in Isaiah. In Israel's most dismal days, Isaiah dared to speak of God's promised deliverance. When the sky is dark, Israel discovered the God who saves. This is only one of the reasons it can be truthfully said that "salvation is from the Jews" (John 4:22) for Israel keeps teaching the world what it means to rely upon God for our ultimate significance.

Old Zechariah is filled with the Holy Spirit when he sees the baby John, cousin of baby Jesus, and sings the Benedictus. There shall be "a mighty savior for us" (Luke 1:69) arising in Israel, a new king,

> to give knowledge of salvation to his people
>   by the forgiveness of their sins.
> By the tender mercy of our God,
>   the dawn from on high will break upon us." (Luke 1:77-78)

New Testament writers are blissfully oblivious to the historical context, details of Jesus' daily life, his adolescent development, his relationship with various socioeconomic groups (all the trivialities that obsess contemporary archaeologists of the "historical Jesus"). With single-minded focus biblical witnesses concentrate only on those matters that are relevant to Jesus as Savior, as if nothing else mattered. Perhaps that's one of the things they want to say—you don't know Jesus if you don't know that he is Savior of the world.

The story of Jesus gives content to the meaning of the word *salvation.* Jesus doesn't speak too often about salvation, rather more typical is for Jesus to talk about the kingdom of God coming near. His message was a simple, one-sentence imperative, "Repent, for the kingdom of heaven has come near" (Matt 4:17; Mark 1:15). God's initiative (kingdom of God) demands human response (repentance and discipleship).

The Greek verb *sōzō* can mean both "to heal" and "to save." Jesus sets things right, rebukes the demons, and stretches out his hand, touches, and commands (Mark 1:41). The demons flee. In places, Jesus heals just by showing up. Jesus enters the picture and demons scream, corpses act up and walk, and the kingdom of God gets real close. "But if it is by the finger of God that I cast out the demons, then the kingdom of God has come to you" (Luke 11:20), *sōzō* incarnate. The scope of Jesus' salvation is extensive, not just uplifting Israel, but providing for nothing less than "the healing of the nations" (Rev 22:2).

Jesus begins his famous sermon with, "Blessed are you who are poor, for yours is the kingdom of God" (Luke 6:20). To those who can do nothing to purchase the kingdom, he gives it to them for nothing. Matthew is not spiritualizing the Beatitudes when he adds poor "in spirit." Poor is poor.

To those who haven't got much spirit, to those who are inept at spiritual matters, who can do little to further their case before God, who by their poverty have no control over their future, Jesus promises everything, his whole glorious kingdom (Matt 5:3).

Is it any wonder then that one of the earliest and most persistent charges against Jesus was, "This fellow welcomes sinners and eats with them" (Luke 15:2)? Jesus is crucified for welcoming sinners to his table, not only welcoming but also actively seeking them. At the end, with whom did he choose to dine at his Last Supper? Sinners. And in his resurrection, at a new beginning, with whom did he choose to dine at his first meals (Luke 24:13-35)? Sinners. His door was too wide to suit many of the faithful.

In the parable of the lost boy (Luke 15), when the boy was "yet far off" the father ran to welcome his prodigal son. The son had a penitent speech prepared for his homecoming, perhaps hoping to ameliorate some of his father's just wrath. The father disallowed the son even to speak. Running to him, he embraced him, welcomed him not simply back home but to an extravagant party, treating him not as the wayward son he was, but as the prince the father intended him to be.

What if the father had simply waited upon the boy? What if the father had not run to meet him? What if the father's forgiving, embracing response were to be made a principle for all our dealings with sin and injustice? Then where would we be? Would there not be moral chaos and parties every night? Is the father's behavior ethically irresponsible?

Let us confine our thought to that which Jesus said, rather than upon idle speculation. Let us cling to the story Jesus tells, as it is. Jesus says that God is like the father who ran to embrace his wayward son and invite him to a party.

Why does the Apostles' Creed so quickly jump from Jesus' birth to his suffering and death, without mention of his teaching or his activity among us? The Apostles' Creed doesn't even say why Jesus came among us, though that may be implied—"Born of the Virgin Mary, suffered under Pontius Pilate," a whole life omitted by a comma!

It's the Nicene Creed that states explicitly that all Christ did and said, including his death and rising, was done "*pro nobis*"—"for us and for our salvation." "Who for us men and our salvation came down from heaven," is how the Nicene Creed characterizes Christ, the Incarnation. To be near us, Christ had to come down to us. There is distance between us and God. We are not with God in heaven, much less are we gods who dwell in the vicinity of deity. Even though we were created by God, in the image of God, God must risk opposition, overcome something, go somewhere in order to come near to us sinners, in order to replenish, restore, and resurrect God's intended image in us. In salvation, God comes, becomes Immanuel, and fully embraces what the human can be. "God with us" is yet another way of thinking about salvation.

John Duns Scotus said that although, in the Incarnation, Jesus died for sinners, God would have become incarnate for us even if we had not sinned, our sin not being the whole point of the Incarnation but rather God's determination to be with us.

In an aside in his *Dogmatics in Outline,* Karl Barth wonders why a political hack like Pontius Pilate made it into our Apostles' Creed. Why do we have to believe in Pilate while we are believing in Jesus? Pilate is affirmed, says Barth, in order to remind us that Jesus is always *hic et nunc* (here and now). Jesus was not some mythological figure who hovered above this grubby, politically infatuated world. Jesus went head-to-head with Pilate over who is in charge. Jesus came to deliver people, to save people from Caesar's power, to transfer their citizenship to another Kingdom. The kingdom of God has come near and, in so doing, rescues people from the grip of politicians. Salvation thus conceived is not simply that which believers receive when they die and go to heaven but rather that present dynamic in which we pass from death to life here and now (1 John 3:14). Salvation is thus a given, decided, present reality, not a yet-to-be-accomplished work of God. "We are not left alone in this frightful world. Into this alien land God has come to us," says Barth.[6] To discover who sits on the throne is yet another way of saying that God is salvation.

In saying that Christ's incarnation was "for our salvation" we see the major reason why the church so strongly asserted that Jesus was truly, fully human. If all we needed for salvation was a helpful moral nudge, then God would have sent a skilled teacher, another Moses to instruct us. If our problem were simply liberation from unjust social structures, God would have surely given another ranting Amos. Knowing that our need was greater than the didactic or the political, the agent of our salvation is both fully divine and fully human; any less complicated a Savior would have been unhelpful.

Salvation is not only what God does in Jesus Christ (what theologians speak of as grace) but also who we are in that converting awareness that God is not only God but also God "for us and for our salvation" (justification and sanctification). When the God who was presumed by us to be an enemy against us is known as God the friend *pro nobis*, that is salvation in its fullness. To be saved is the fitting human response to the stunning divine move on us. This is why Peter can say to the street mob, "Save yourselves from this corrupt generation" (Acts 2:40). Though we are not the agents of salvation, God's salvation is meant to be received, embraced, and enjoyed.

THE GOSPEL OF SALVATION

What is the gospel? Karl Barth says that when we say "gospel," good news, we are talking about salvation, about the mighty acts that God has worked *pro nobis*:

> The gospel is constituted by the mighty acts of God in history for the liberation of the cosmos. It is not a set of rickety arguments about the divine order; it is not the expression of some sublime religious experience brought mysteriously to verbal form; it is not a romantic report about awareness of God in nature; it is not a speculative, philosophical theory about the nature of ultimate reality; it is not a set of pious or moral maxims designed to straighten out the world; it is not a legalistic lament about the meanness of human nature; it is not a sentimental journey down memory lane into ancient history. It is the unique narrative of what God has done to inaugurate [God's] kingdom in Jesus of Nazareth, crucified outside Jerusalem, risen from the dead, seated at the right hand of God, and now reigning eternally with the Father, through the activity of the Holy Spirit, in the church and in the world. Where this is not announced, it will not be known. [7]

Barth says what the gospel is not—not religious experience, not moral platitudes, not an attempt to straighten out the world, not a deeper appreciation of nature, not something personal and subjective, not ancient history—in order to say that salvation is "the mighty acts of God in history for the liberation of the cosmos." The first book of the Bible says that the world is initiated solely through an act of God and the last book of the Bible is a sustained hymn that sings the great triumph of God in which creatures in heaven and on earth sing that "salvation belongs to our God who is seated on the throne" (Rev 7:10). Crucified Jesus is the one who brings, "Salvation and glory and power" (Rev 19:1).

A Christian is someone who lives in the light of this story. A Christian and a Buddhist (or for that matter, a Republican or a Democrat) differ primarily on the basis of the stories they are living. These stories tell us what is going on in the world, what we might reasonably expect and who really sits on the throne.

We could never have made this story up by ourselves, "this salvation of God" (Acts 28:28). We thought we knew what salvation was until we were face to face with the Christ, God's definition of salvation. Salvation does not mean anything we would like it to mean. Salvation has a particular face, a specific name, a location. We might have liked to be saved in Switzerland, which is a beautiful place. Instead, God reveals our salvation in a dusty, utterly unappealing locale (ugly back then and still is) like Nazareth. We might have received our salvation more gladly had it come to us more generally as the highest and best of humanity rather than specifically as a Jew from Nazareth who was tortured to death.

Salvation is learning to live with the God that we've got, now and forever, learning to love the God who saves. You can easily see that the thing that impresses me, as a Wesleyan, about the God we've got is that *God is love*. Of course, the statement, *God is love*, is problematic. For one thing, we don't know God. For another thing, our talk of love is suspect. Both the word *God* and the word *love* await content and definition by the particular stories that are Scripture.

We must therefore attend to Scripture, listening carefully, enjoying the particulars, looking for the overall picture that emerges, so that we may know the God that we've got, or, more specifically to the way the Scripture tells it, the God who has got us. (Remember that you are reading the thoughts of one who, when asked by a bishop the traditional ordination question, "Are you convinced that everything necessary for salvation is contained in the scriptures of Old and New Testaments?" answered, "yes.")

A good place to begin is with attention to one of Jesus' greatest hits, the so-called good Samaritan (Luke 10). A man on his way from Jerusalem to Jericho is victimized by thieves who rob him, beat him, and leave him half dead and in the ditch. Down the road comes a priest. This officially religious man will surely be the salvation for the man in the ditch. No, the priest passes by on the other side. If the clergy won't save you, who will? Then comes a pious, Bible-believing layperson—who passes by on the other side. Last comes a despised Samaritan. You have lost a lot of blood. This is your ultimate hope for rescue but you are aghast to learn that your hope, your salvation is none other than a good-for-nothing, anything-but-poor-and-pious, lousy Samaritan.

"I'm OK," you protest. "It's just a flesh wound. Don't bother yourself," muttering under your breath, "I'd rather die in this ditch than to be saved by the likes of you!"

The loathed Samaritan risks all, extravagantly responds to the need of the man in the ditch. So this is not a story about a person who stops and gives the man in the ditch the use of his cell phone in order to call the highway patrol—we would have done that. It's a story about the odd, threatening, humiliating, and extravagant form by which God draws near to us for our rescue. And, in noting our reaction to the story, it's a story about our shock at the peculiar One who risked all for us.

Like most of Scripture, the story of the man in the ditch is a story about God before it is a story about us, about the oddness of our salvation in Christ. I've used this interpretation of the parable of the good Samaritan before, and I can tell you that my congregation didn't like it. They like stories about themselves more than they like to hear stories about God. They are resourceful, educated, gifted people who don't like to be cast in the role of the beaten poor man in the ditch. They would rather be the anything-but-poor Samaritan who does something nice for the less fortunate among us. In other words, they don't like to admit that just possibly they may need to be saved.

Why is this story not about us? Doesn't the story end with Jesus saying to his interrogator, "Go and do likewise"? "Go" and "do" what? I'm saying that more difficult even than reaching out to the victim in the ditch (which is hard enough for us) is coming to conceive of yourself as the victim, learning to live as if your one last hope is the Savior whom you tend to despise. [8]

The Samaritan is more than a moralistic story about how we ought to do good for others but rather a joke about how Jesus makes all of us look poor and beaten up and then teaches us to receive the God we've got. When Jesus was criticized for the company he kept at table, he was clear that he saves only the abandoned and the dying (Luke 19:10). But that also means that we can expect some resistance to the notion that Jesus Christ is *our* salvation. In John's Gospel we looked upon Immanuel, God with us, and cried, "you are a Samaritan and have a demon" (John 8:48). Many looked upon God's salvation—a Jew from Nazareth who lived briefly, died violently, and rose unexpectedly—and responded, "We would rather die in the ditch than to be saved by you." Therefore, the story of our salvation is, at key points, a story of our resistance, our violence to the Savior we did not expect.

Jesus reacts to our situation in the ditch, not with more rules and regulations, not with harsh condemnation, but with a sort of love that can only be called reckless, extravagant, prodigal. There is, dare I say it, a kind of promiscuous quality in his extroverted love.

When asked, by someone like me, "What must I do to inherit eternal life?" Jesus said, "Go, sell what you own, and give the money to the poor" (Mark 10:21). This was a ridiculously extravagant demand, except this is exactly what Jesus himself was soon to do on the cross.

"And if anyone wants to sue you and take your coat, give your cloak as well; and if anyone forces you to go one mile, go also the second mile. Give to everyone who begs from you, and do not refuse anyone who wants to borrow from you" (Matt 5:40-42). Note that Jesus has not defined love as bringing out the best in other people, or love as making the world a better place in which to live, nor is love something that comes naturally from good people like us. Love is more demanding than a pagan virtue like justice. Jesus' love is what Jesus commands, something enabled by who he is. He expended everything. He laid down his life for a bunch of stupid, wayward sheep, friends who were also his betrayers.

In so doing, Jesus was not simply being a great ethical teacher; one is impressed by the impracticality of what Jesus commands. If you give everything you've got to the poor, eventually you will have nothing to give. And how does self-giving better the lot of the poor after they have consumed everything that you have given? Will such liberality only produce character flaws in the poor? If you so thoughtlessly give to the needs of others in this way, you will eventually be used by others who will take advantage of you. Taken to the extreme, it could lead to your death.

But then Jesus says that this is exactly where this should lead. "No one has greater love than this, to lay down one's life for one's friends" (John 15:13). Love, as Jesus embodies love, is reckless self-expenditure. "If any want to become my followers, let them deny themselves and take up their cross daily and follow me" (Luke 9:23).

Why would Jesus commend such a way? He seems to do so, not because of its potential human benefits and rewards, but simply because *this is the way God is.* This is the way reality is. This is the grain of the universe. He is thereby revealing the way the world is meant to be, all the way down. Without consideration of benefits or consequences, this is reality. A seed can only germinate and come to fruition when it falls to the earth and dies (John 12:24). Being most fully alive, being most completely who we are created to be, is a matter of self-expenditure. Self-giving is self-fulfillment. Whosoever loses a life, finds life. "Whoever does not love abides in death" (1 John 3:14). The greatest of all is servant of all. Whoever wants to become great must turn and become as nothing but a little child.

"This is my commandment, that you love one another as I have loved you" (John 15:12). And as 1 John puts it, "We know love by this, that he laid down his life for us—and we ought to lay down our lives for one another" (1 John 3:16). Jesus was "in the form of God . . . taking the form of a slave . . . he humbled himself and became obedient to the point of death" (Phil 2:6-8).

This way is *the* way? This puts in context Jesus' words that he is "the way, and the truth, and the life. No one comes to the Father except through me" (John 14:6).

"This is eternal life, that they may know you, the only true God, and Jesus Christ whom you have sent" (John 17:3). What the Savior revealed is not just God in general, deity in the abstract—that is, a God without soteriological punch—but a very particular, very peculiar kind of God, a God who is, in a number of essential ways, most "ungodlike." Here is no "god" who divinely floats above the grubby realities of this world but rather a God who, in love, locates *pro nobis.*

Thus Karl Barth said, "God is the God of the eternal election of His grace." [9] Scripture tells us that which we could never know on our own, namely that God has elected to be our God not only at the beginning but also at the end. God has decided, in grace, to be for us. This is not only something that God sometimes does, or once did; this is who God is now, God *pro nobis.* The whole doctrine of the Trinity is our attempt to name the God who has met us in Jesus Christ. Jesus Christ was not just an aspect of God or a good indicator of God; he was God. In him the fullness of God was pleased to dwell, all of the glory of God in him.

And our reaction to such close-quartered glory? In unison we cried, "Crucify him!"

God knows we tried to forget this story or to supplant it with alternative salvific accounts. Every story counter to Scripture tends to be an attempt to be done with that God who refuses to be done with us. I just heard the sermon of a TV preacher (who preaches each Sunday to more people than I preach to in a year). Though his sermon was charmingly delivered, his message was one of autosalvation—you are a good person who, with the right principles in your head (which I will tell you), by the application of the right technique (which I have discovered and will now graciously give you), will be able to save yourself by yourself.

The preacher didn't actually use the word *save,* for I doubt that he thinks we're in any kind of dilemma from which we need to be saved. (Improvement, rather than salvation, seemed to be his goal.) Nor did he refer to Scripture in his sermon, which seemed wise since the story he was attempting to lay over our lives is meant (even if he doesn't know it) to defeat the story that is Scripture. I don't think he even used the name "God"—his sanguine account of the human condition really doesn't leave any work for God to do that we cannot just as well do for ourselves. Surely, his sermon implies, there is some means for us to get saved other than by Jesus.

CREATION CONTINUED

Plato noted, and Freud reiterated, that the human animal, from the first, seems to have this insatiable longing, this great yearning. The infant demands attention from the world, insists on being noticed. The human is a fragile animal who cannot survive alone, who must make connection first with the mother, then with one human being after another. Plato said that this was the beginning of all human thought and culture, the explanation for all human achievement, and much human misery too. We must connect.

Yet here's the great mystery: *The God of Israel and the church also connects.* It is not so much that God *must* connect but there is something about this God that seems, from the first, exuberantly to desire us, to want to communicate with us, abundantly to self-reveal to us. God's generativity doesn't end with Genesis 1. The kingdom of God comes near. In his *Miscellanies*, Jonathan Edwards marvels that though the Son is the complete, self-sufficient image of the Father who wants for nothing, the Son is for us a vivid sign of the Father's determination never to be completely alone. Edwards says, "The Son has an inclination to communicate himself, . . . and this was the end of creation, even the communication of the happiness of the Son of God. . . . And [humanity] . . . is the immediate subject of this."[10] The point of the whole world is to be the Creator's dialogue partner in conversation, in connection. Calvin said that God could have created us for God's usefulness but the great thing about God is God created us for God's sheer delight.[11] God delights in having conversation partners, even poor dialogue partners like us. The Revealer who delights in revelation desires recipients for the revelation. So a first response to the question, "Who shall be saved?" might be, "Well, who is created? What creatures are so beloved by the Creator that the Creator cannot let them alone? Who is God's favorite conversation partner? These are the ones God saves."

Will you accept this as a fair summary of much of Scripture—God's got this thing for us? God is determined—through Creation, the sagas of the Patriarchs, the words of the prophets, the teaching of the law, and the birth and death of the Christ—to get close, very close, too close for comfort, in fact. Sorry, if you thought when we said "God" we had in mind an impersonal power, a fair-minded, balanced bureaucrat who is skilled in the dispassionate administration of natural law from a safe distance in eternity. Our God is intensely, unreservedly personal. The God of Israel and the church refuses to be an abstraction or a generality. In the Bible, God gets angry, repents, threatens, promises, punishes, takes back, and resumes the conversation. Only persons do such things and, when we do them, it is a sign of our personal worth, the highest of our personhood, our passionate valuing of something over nothing, not of our grubby anthropocentric imperfection.

The most important decision in Christian theology is to decide whether you will speak of God as a person or as a concept, as a name or as an idea. Talk about God as, to use Paul Tillich's term, "ultimate reality," and you will get a safe, dead abstraction that you can utilize in whatever salvation project you happen now to be working. Name God as Father, Son, and Holy Spirit, and God will enlist you in God's move upon the world. That's one of the things we mean when we say that "Jesus is Lord" or "Jesus is God's only Son." This God is shockingly personal, available, and present. It's also what we mean when we say that "Jesus is Savior." This is in no way detraction from the Father's immense deity. There are gods who could not risk getting close. We are killers who tend to resent our would-be saviors. Anybody who would love me risks great pain because of me. So most "gods" are careful to keep their distance through abstraction and idealization. "Gods" are, by definition, distant, high, and lifted up.

The one whom Israel calls Yahweh and the church knows as Trinity is so great as to be utterly personal, available, and richly present to us. This God is against detached reserve. "God never rests," says Luther, constantly pursuing, presenting to us. You can't get much closer to us, to the real us, than a cross.

Christians are witnesses to a great cosmic incursion, an invasion in which God, rather than being distant from the world, has daringly entered the world (Gal 4:4). The world is God's contested territory in a vast program of reclamation.

Furthermore, God not only refuses to be God alone, not only makes a move on Pilate and on all the principalities and powers of this world but also enlists us in God's salvific work. Whereas God is author and agent of our salvation, God refuses to work alone. John Wesley shocked the Calvinists and Lutherans of his day by asserting divine-human synergy in our salvation. God graciously saves us *and* graciously invites our active participation in the drama of salvation. Salvation and vocation are thus linked.

Consider the story in Exodus 32, the golden calf. While Moses receives the Ten Commandments upon the mountain, down in the valley his brother Aaron violates the First Commandment by offering a golden calf as a means of salvation. (Exodus mocks such idolatry—some pagans worshiped the fertility of the sacred bull—the best Aaron and the Israelites could muster is a mere sacred calf!) The author of the First Commandment is understandably furious at this act of blatant disobedience and threatens punishment.

When Moses pleads in behalf of the wayward Israelites, God refuses to be placated, telling Moses, "Now let me alone, so that my wrath may burn" (Exod 32:10). Moses continues to beg, arguing with God for the sake of his people. Amazingly, God's rage is for a time held in check due to Moses' pleading, even though Moses is not the most eloquent of public speakers. We see this sort of dialogue elsewhere, with Abraham, with Jeremiah, and with Job. The God of Scripture is not an impersonal, absolute sovereign with whom there is no argument. God is free to be dissuaded, free to be in conversation even with a tongue-tied earthling like Moses, free to change God's mind and repent, because God is determined to be God for us, determined to be the means of our salvation.

At certain key moments, Scripture is thus a kind of dialogue, not by equal partners, but still a dialogue that is God's grace. We must therefore be suspicious of abstract, impersonal, generic notions of God that make abstract claims that God is omnipotent, utterly free, and transcendent. Abstractions mean nothing apart from the specific narratives of Scripture that tell us what true power, freedom, and transcendence look like now that God looks like a crucified and resurrected Jew from Nazareth. God is the loving Father, Son, and Holy Spirit whose great sovereignty is that self-elected freedom to be in conversation, even free to be dissuaded by the pleas of someone like Moses, in order to be who God really is—God *pro nobis.*

When Christians say that God is "transcendent," this is what we are trying to say. The hiddenness and distance of God are precisely in God's nearby self-revelation as God on the cross. God's difference from our expectations for gods makes God hidden to us. We are resistant to the near God on the cross because of our assumption that if there were a true God, that God would be somewhere a long way from us, not here before us, naked, exposed and bleeding, certainly not one with us, not *pro nobis*. A righteous God would be aloof from us sinners, certainly not intrude through our locked doors (John 20) to show us his hands full of holes and to make us touch the gash in his side, to breathe his Holy Spirit upon us and thereby make his betrayers also his Body, his church, this God resurrected *pro nobis*.

Scripture's curious story of salvation is the story of a God who makes a world and delightedly calls it "good," though the Creation gives little indication—right from the first, with its fratricide and relentless head bashing—that the Creator's verdict is accurate. From the majestic cadences of Genesis 1, "Let there be," "and God saw that it was good." everything tends to go downhill once we go to work. The Creator has something other in mind, in calling all life into being and calling it "good" than what the Creator gets. Disobedience, rebellion, and blood are what the creature has in mind, "from youth" (Gen 8:21). And though the Creator gets angry, wreaks wrath, and storms off in a huff from time to time, for some reason the Creator keeps coming back to the creature, keeps resuming the conversation, keeps working with the creature who is, despite periodic bouts of good intention, hostile toward the very same God who gives life.

Because the story continues beyond our first rebellion in Genesis, we see that salvation is what God does from the beginning: "all things have been created through him and for him" (Col 1:16). Salvation is not some tactic that God had to devise after the disaster of our first rebellion in the Garden, God's Plan B after we failed to follow Plan A in Eden. From the beginning, we are created for oneness with God and what God does with us, from the beginning, is atonement, at-one-ment.

At a youth conference, the leader stood and read from Paul's Letter to the Romans:

> For while we were still weak, at the right time Christ died for the ungodly. Indeed, rarely will anyone die for a righteous person—though perhaps for a good person someone might actually dare to die. But God proves his love for us in that while we were still sinners Christ died for us . . . we have been justified by his blood, . . . saved through him from the wrath of God. For if while we were enemies, we were reconciled to God through the death of his Son, much more surely, having been reconciled, will we be saved by his life. (Rom 5:6-10)

"I need your help," the speaker told the youth. "Who wants to be in a skit of Romans 5?" Hands were raised.

"OK, on the stage is a continuum from the very bad, on my left, to the very good, on my right. On my left is complete evil and on my right is complete good. As you are called to the stage, I want you to place yourself where you belong in regard to the good and the bad. OK? Now who will be Mother Teresa?"

A teenager went up and took her place on the far right.

"Martin Luther King?" Another came up and stood just to the left of Mother Teresa.

"Mahatma Gandhi?" The three of them hung out on the right edge.

"OK, next, Adolph Hitler?" A young man grinningly took his proper place on the far left, all the way across stage from the three saints.

"Osama bin Laden? Attila the Hun?" Other villains came up and dutifully clustered on the far left.

"Now, I need one more person up here—Jesus Christ. Jesus, come on up," he said. Eventually a young woman was coaxed forward. Mother Teresa, Martin Luther King, and Gandhi politely gave way as Jesus moved to the extreme right.

The speaker looked out on the assembled youth and exclaimed, "Do you people not listen? Did you not pay attention when I read the scripture? I'll read this one more time."

He flipped open his Bible and began to read, "At the right time Christ died for the ungodly," and as he read Jesus sheepishly moved away from Mother Teresa and Martin Luther King, across the stage, over to where Osama bin Laden and the others received him.

When he finished reading from Romans, the speaker said into the shocked silence, "Now, is there anybody here with the guts to come up and stand with Jesus and to walk with Jesus into your school on Monday morning? Anybody here open to that sort of salvation?"

Dozens of youth streamed forward, eager to give themselves to the one who, while we were still weak, at the right time, gave himself for the ungodly.

Spoken toward the end of Scripture, this could have been said every step of the way from the first, "I will be their God and they will be my children" (Rev 21:7). The once ungodly will be the godly. Salvation is when God finally gets what God wants in creating the world. Salvation means finally, safely to arrive where you have always been intended by God to be. One might expect God's restored good creation to be a redeemed garden to make up for the paradise we botched up in Genesis. Instead, Revelation says that God's crowning act of restoration is communitarian: New Jerusalem, a populous, raucously singing city, rather than a serene garden. You get this sort of result from a God who loves a crowd:

> Then the angel showed me the river of the water of life, bright as crystal, flowing from the throne of God and of the Lamb through the middle of the street of the city. On either side of the river is the tree of life with its twelve kinds of fruit, producing its fruit each month; and the leaves of the tree are for the healing of the nations. Nothing accursed will be found there any more. But the throne of God and of the Lamb will be in it, and his servants will worship him; they will see his face, and his name will be on their foreheads. And there will be no more night; they need no light of lamp or sun, for the Lord God will be their light, and they will reign forever and ever. (Rev 22:1-5)

CHAPTER TWO

THE EROS OF GOD

"Who will be saved?" is not as interesting a question as "Who saves?" That which makes Christian salvation counterintuitive, counter-cultural, and strange is the God who saves.

I saw this in the great mosaic apse at the church in Monreale, Sicily, a wonder of the medieval world. There, presiding over a dazzling array of jewel-like depictions of the story of our salvation is Christ Pantocrator—Christ, Creator of all. Having seen photographs of that apse, I expected to be be-dazzled by the Byzantine otherness of Christ, Christ the Judge of humanity. And yet the Christ I saw was Christ of the wide embrace, hands out-stretched, reaching out from his majesty as if to encircle the whole church, the whole creation in his reach. All the stories of Scripture—told with such vitality and wonder in the mosaics of Monreale—are vignettes of this grand vision of a God who is stubbornly determined to have all of humanity.

Leaving the church at Monreale, a street vendor held up a trinket with Christ's picture stamped upon it. "Don't you want to take a little Jesus with you, mister?" he asked. No, we don't take Christ with us; he takes us places.

God's intended oneness, because of our sin, ended in a crucifixion; yet even in the Crucifixion, God is not thwarted. God creatively weaves such tragedy into God's purposes thereby remaking our sin into God's great tri-umphant embrace. "If we are faithless, he remains faithful—for he cannot deny himself," says 2 Timothy 2:13. The best modifier of this God is "love."

This God seems to have a desire to have us that is erotic in intensity. We make a mistake to separate *agape* from *eros* in speaking of the love that is experienced as the Trinity. Who is the lover in the Song of Songs?

> Upon my bed at night
>   I sought him whom my soul loves;
> I sought him, but found him not;
>   I called him, but he gave no answer.

> I will rise now and go about the city,
>   in the streets and in the squares;
> I will seek him whom my soul loves."
>   I sought him, but found him not.
> The sentinels found me,
>   as they went about in the city.
> "Have you seen him whom my soul loves?"
> Scarcely had I passed them,
>   when I found him whom my soul loves.
> I held him, and would not let him go
>   until I brought him into my mother's house,
> and into the chamber of her that conceived me. (Song 3:1-4)

The church has traditionally taught that this Hebrew love song, which at first appears to be the erotic thoughts of two heated adolescents, is actually an allegory of the love of Christ for his church. Isn't it scandalous that the closest analogy for the love of God in Christ is the infatuated, sensual ramblings of two adolescents consumed with lust—I mean *love*—for each other? Love is costly, consuming, and fanatical, says the Song of Solomon. Apparently, God has got this thing for us almost like lust. Just before being hung by the Nazis in Tegel Prison, Bonhoeffer wrote to his friend Bethge that he had been meditating on, of all the books of the Bible, the Song of Solomon and found there much strong comfort that "nothing calamitous can happen" when we are loved by such an "ardent, passionate, sensual love that is portrayed there."[1] Nothing calamitous—even as catastrophic as the Nazis—can happen to the person who has been ravished, claimed, embraced by such salvific love.

It is scandalous too that the New Testament dares to call the poor old church Christ's "bride." The church is invited by God to do what husbands and wives do in marriage. The bride nervously awaits the full consummation of Christ's love, recipient of a kind of arranged marriage. She is besmirched, unworthy of such adoration by one so pure and good. Still, she knows that she is betrothed, spoken for by the Savior who will keep his promise to fulfill his passionate intention to make love to sinners (Rev 21:2, 9). Jesus looks upon the poor old church the way a proper groom looks upon his bride.

God erotically risks, desires union with humanity. So God comes close enough to be not only God for us but also God with us. In what biblical writers call "the fullness of time" God steps up, steps in, and steps out in a most amazing overture of love. The God who was from the first so joyously creative extends that divine creativity to become Incarnate. A defiant young woman (Mary) submits to be a fellow conspirator in God's dramatic, miraculous move on humanity (Luke 1:46-55). Swept up in God's invasion of God's world, she bears a son with the revealing name, "God is with us" (Matt 1:23).

Think of all those images in John's Gospel where Jesus stresses intimacy. He not only comes to us but "abides" with us. He is the shepherd, and we are the sheep; he the vine, we the branches. Bread, we are to feed upon him. He is the Water of Life who eternally quenches our thirst. Almost never does this God seek simple agreement or correct thinking. God seeks us, all of us. God's goal for us is intimacy, indwelling. Not I, "but . . . Christ who lives in me," said Paul (Gal 2:20).

In Islam, at least from my amateurish reading of the Qur'an, there is this constant distancing of God, apparently as a means of honoring God. The God who is rendered in Islam is noble and exalted, at some remove from the world, God as absolute and majestic as a god can get. You would have to know the incarnational story that I've just narrated to know why that's a problem. Christians don't know that God is sovereign, noble, exalted, absolute, high, and lifted up. We know that God is Immanuel, love with us, for us.

By the way, we do not take it as a compliment that Islam regards Jesus as a great prophet. Jesus is a prophet, but prophets, even the most truthful and courageous of them, cannot save. They can announce salvation, but they can't do it. Jesus is not just preparing us for the last prophet, Muhammad; Jesus redeems us so that we are free to stop awaiting prophets to tell us what to do because a Savior has already acted in our behalf. Jesus is not simply the one who shows the way; he is the way (John 14:6). It appears that Muslims think of the Qur'an in the same way that we think of Jesus. (I'll admit that there are some Christians whose fundamentalist views of Scripture are more akin to Islam than to Orthodox Christianity.) The Holy Qur'an, recited by Muhammad, is the way that Muslims get to a sovereign, majestic, exalted God who intersects history. The Crucifixion, so vehemently denied by the Qur'an[2] (for it is outrageous for a true prophet to suffer such a fate) is for Christians a window into the heart of God. When we see God next to us, stooped toward us, in the muck and mire with us in order to have us, that's what Christians call God.

The biblical testimony of God as the waiting father, the passionate lover is difficult for us because as modern people we are creations of the Enlightenment. During the Enlightenment, the individual was invented as the sovereign, supreme center of reality. Human beings were said to be most fully developed when they are most completely self-sufficient, self-made, and self-reliant. The truly developed person learns to shed social connections and restraints and stand alone, stripped of relations. From a Christian point of view, in the Enlightenment the modern self did not grow; it shrank. The thin contemporary self, a creation of the individual's choices of the moment, responsible only for itself, having no greater project than itself was the self shed of the very qualities that previously were thought to be most humane. Therefore, to be told that salvation is tethered to a God who connects, a God whose Trinitarian nature is inherently relational, communitarian, and communicative, is to encounter a God who appears to be against everything in which we believe. There is a reason why there is no God in the *Harry Potter* novels. Potter is not only good entertainment but also training in how to get by in the modern world alone, yet with an active imagination.

Christians have the intellectual means for devising one of the most pessimistic assessments of human nature. We really do believe that all of us, *all*, are sinners, all the way down, gleefully on our way to hell in a handbasket. Believing this enabled me to say—when George W. Bush told us that we were going into Iraq for the very best of motives to do the very best of work—"Probably not." When told that the purpose of our war was "Enduring Freedom," I responded, "Probably not." By the way, belief in the persistence of sin also enabled me to say (quietly, to myself), when someone said that I was one of the most selfless, godly bishops ever, "Probably not."

We are able to be pessimistic about human motives and achievements (most especially our own) because we are optimistic about the ultimate triumph of a God who saves the ungodly. Ephesians says that we are as good as dead but that, in our salvation, God pulls off nothing less than resurrection. Confidence in the salvific triumph of God enables us to tell the truth about us. We are sad, scary beings, but God,

> who is rich in mercy, out of the great love with which he loved us even when we were dead through our trespasses, made us alive together with Christ—by grace you have been saved—and raised us up with him and seated us with him in the heavenly places in Christ Jesus, so that in the ages to come he might show the immeasurable riches of his grace in kindness toward us in Christ Jesus. For by grace you have been saved through faith, and this is not of your own doing; it is the gift of God. (Eph 2:4-8)

For most of the people to whom I've preached, the most challenging words in this Pauline passage are that salvation "is not of your own doing; it is the gift of God." Reasonably well fixed, fairly well off, mostly successful in getting anything we want through our checkbooks, we are surprised that there is anything, including our situation with God, that is not the result of our own doing, anything that is pure gift, grace. As Scripture teaches, "salvation is from the Jews" (John 4:22). Salvation is not what we desire or earn. We must, therefore, submit to Scripture, must bow to Jews and their testimony; we must allow ourselves to be welcomed into the salvific promises of God to Israel.

Creation implies donation. In a world that is created, all is gift. This is a difficult truth for those of us who are modern and who have, therefore, been taught to believe that all good is an achievement of our sole fabrication. Knowledge is reduced to power, a possession, the accumulation of which enables us better to dominate the world. Plato (and Augustine) taught that in order really to know something, the would-be knower must be willingly seduced by the object of knowing, to fall in love with what is to be known, to enjoy erotic participation in the object of our knowing. We, however, want to know in order to dominate, to use. In a world of utility, there is paucity of gratitude and little real joy.

God help you if you try to think about a gratuitous matter like salvation in this utilitarian way. Christians are taught to believe that everything is only what we have been given. Augustine was fond of quoting 1 Corinthians 4:7 which he translates as, "What do you have that you haven't received? And if you have received it, why boast as if you hadn't?"

Salvation, from our side, is acceptance rather than decision, result, or program because salvation is, in the words of Paul, "free gift":

> The grace of the one man, Jesus Christ, abounded for the many. . . . If, because of the one man's trespass [Adam], death exercised dominion through that one, much more surely will those who receive the abundance of grace and the free gift of righteousness exercise dominion in life through the one man, Jesus Christ. (Rom 5:15, 17)

Note that Paul uses the more passive "receive" (*lambano*) rather than the more active "decide" or "choose," stressing the work of Christ rather than our decision. When asked, "Where were you saved?" Barth replied, "On Golgotha."

To glory in salvation as a possession, to boast of it as something achieved and now owned, is to show that one is fundamentally confused.

C. S. Lewis speaks of his conversion to Christ as an act that God worked in him that was almost coercive in its effect, that time when "God closed in on me" and he came to the cross as "a prodigal who is brought in kicking, struggling, resentful, and darting his eyes in every direction as a chance for escape." [3]

ETERNAL LIFE

It is this miraculous, gifted quality of salvation that is lacking in popular pagan views of death and the afterlife. Most people I know believe in the "immortality of the soul"—there is in us a divine spark that goes on and on even after our physical death. That's Plato, not Paul. Greeks like Plato taught that human beings possess an immortal, imperishable "soul" that goes on, in some shadowy sense, beyond the ravages of physical death.

"I believe that my daughter has now become the rain, the wind moving in the trees, the stars that shine in the night," said a woman to me after her daughter died of leukemia. I'm sure that her notion of immortality was comforting to the grieving mother. And yet, I feared that it would ultimately turn out to be false comfort. First, it seemed to me a sad denial of the horror and the tragedy of a young woman's death. Wind moving through the trees is small potatoes compared with a living, breathing, loving, adorable person. Paul said that death is hated, the "final enemy" (1 Cor 15:26), and I believe him right. Second, wind moving through the trees is leftover small change compared with the treasure of a distinct, embodied, personality whom we have known and loved, loved not so much for her general humanity, but loved personally in her delightful particularity. I feared that this grieving mother was settling for too little. But mine is a point of view prejudiced by Christian salvation.

Christians believe that nothing about us is eternal. As X. J. Kennedy's poetic, washed-out whore says, "For when Time takes you out for a spin in his car / You'll be hard-pressed to keep him from going too far." [4] When we die, we die. We don't just appear to be snuffed out, then to sail forth into some vague metaphysical, shadowy state. We return to the dust from which we came. Tears and wailing are appropriate responses from loved ones when the sting of death strikes their beloved. And yet, in a spectacular miracle of God, the same God who raised dead Jesus somehow reaches in, defeats the enemy death, and takes us along as well. Jesus was resurrected into some new "body" whereby he appeared to his disciples in his resurrected state. It was a very different body—he could walk through doors, appear and disappear to his disciples. They did not readily recognize him in his resurrected body but still, after a few bodily acts—like touching him and eating with him—they recognized him as the same Jesus whom they loved, followed, and at times disobeyed, although he was Jesus in a wonderfully different form. Yet there is even more. The bold claim of his disciples was not only that Jesus was raised, but he promised to reach in and resurrect them as well. "Because I live," said Jesus, "you'll live too." So John Calvin spoke of our reconciliation to God as "vivification," restored to God, we are vivified.

Immortality is attractive because it acts as if eternality is something that we possess as human beings. Resurrection is humbling because it is pure gift to utterly mortal beings like us. Immortality usually assumes continuity in the next life with this life—if we enjoyed rose gardening in this life, we'll get to garden in the next. Resurrection promises a whole new world, a radical discontinuity with the pain and frustration of life in this world, discontinuity that occurs because we are now near God in a healed, restored, wonderfully refashioned world.

Why does my church talk so little about salvation? We preachers speak before people who neither conceive of themselves as dying down in the ditch nor know a God who is able to stoop, a God who not only loves to heal, but loves even to raise the dead. Able to solve most of our real problems by ourselves, fairly well off and well fixed, working out regularly and watching our diets, we come to church only for helpful suggestions for saving ourselves. As Jesus would have said of someone in our circumstances, "You've already had your reward" (Luke 16:9-18).

I'm reminded of that dramatic moment in the Exodus when Moses tells Israel "stand firm, and see the deliverance that the LORD will accomplish" (Exod 14:13). "Thus the LORD saved Israel that day" (14:30). Note that all that is required of us is to stand and to see. The rest is God's. God forbid that this book be written or read as just another of our salvation projects. Better that these pages be part of our standing, seeing, and adoring the salvation of the Lord.

God may be *pro nobis*, for us, but God is also *extra nos*, outside us. Whether we know it, like it, respond to it or not, something has occurred in Jesus Christ that is not determined by us nor limited by the boundaries of our imagination. We must not make the effectiveness of God's work on the cross and in the Resurrection contingent on human responsiveness. The reality of salvation by Christ precedes any human possibility of salvation in Christ. Redemption is an accomplished fact, *pro nobis*. But God's determination fully to have us and completely to love us makes this an event also *in nobis*. Though reconciliation with God is a gift of God, it has yet to be fully accomplished until God gets all that God wants—to have us, all of us, in communion. Salvation is the good news, "Become who, by the grace of God, you really are" rather than the bad news, "Try hard to be someone who, with enough strenuous spiritual effort, you might eventually be."

Thus there is a finished and completed quality about the work of God on the cross. Yet by the grace of God, there is "more and even more" as well, as we find ourselves drawn daily into the sphere of such love, as we grow in our ability to return some of the love that has so completely, fully loved us. Salvation is not a project to be done by us but a gift to be received by us. Gratitude, responsiveness becomes a fundamental motif of the Christian life. Although our "yes" does not accomplish our salvation, our little yes is given a place in the fulfillment of God's great "Yes!" to us in the cross and resurrection of Christ. And the Wesleyan in me suspects that our "yes" will rarely be a one-time, once and for all "yes."

God's love desires not only our assent but also our participation. Jesus doesn't just want us to adore him but to follow him. We are told by Jesus that we are to take up his cross daily (Luke 9:23). Every day we must wake up, jump out of bed, and be surprised by the scope of our salvation in Christ. Our "yes" thus becomes "yes" again-and-again, more-and-more as we grow in grace. As Barth said, we are all "amateurs" when it comes to our faith in Christ. We keep having these fine moments of recognition and recognition in which we once again are "surprised by joy" (C. S. Lewis). In the Lord's Prayer, note that we again and again, as if for the first time, ask God for the gift of our *daily* bread.

The smug "I'm saved, how about you?" betrays the grace of God as a daily, ongoing, continually awakening, and surprising gift of emergent awareness. We are *saved* by the completed work of Christ, yet it is also true that we are graciously, moment-by-moment *being saved*. We thus may joyfully anticipate that time, that place when we shall be fully "saved," closer to the heart of God than we ever dreamed or dared imagine. Paul says that he, and indeed the whole creation, is "groaning" in agony for such complete redemption (Rom 8:22).

If you've never known what it's like to be offered the gift of love by another person, I'm too poor a poet to describe it for you. But if you have been so loved, you'll know what the church is pointing to when it describes the grace of God as unmerited, life-giving, life-transforming gift, almost like the *eros* of two adolescents.

The church has always struggled to interact divine initiative (God's initiating "Yes") with human agency (human responding "yes"), God's objective work on the cross and our subjective response. Christ's presence in the Eucharist, the church has said, is always valid and efficacious, no matter how poorly performed by the priest, though not always beneficial to the recipient because of the demeanor of the recipient. It is this objective quality of God's work that has been smothered in our contemporary subjectivity. North American evangelical Christianity has unfortunately tended to speak of salvation in a way that makes it sound as if it were a psychological experience that we have rather than a work that God does. Barth said that our reconciliation to God is a present actuality, a fact that has been established by the work of God, not something that we think we have experienced.

Salvation comes to the empty-handed. "Just as I am without one plea, but that thy blood was shed for me," as we sing. The church is not here to produce a product—to *make* disciples, *produce* converts, or *win* people to Christ (note the capitalist metaphors). God in Christ is already doing that. We are simply (did I say *simply*?) to point to this particular God, to testify to what has happened in the invasion of our humanity by this God, and to show the world what life looks like when a life submits to the realty of Christ. We have been shown something that much of the world is waiting to see, even when the world doesn't yet know for whom it awaits.

Once upon a time I went out to a small rural church to baptize a twelve-year-old boy whom a pastor had been instructing in the faith. I was happy to oblige until the pastor said, "Jeremy very much wants to be immersed. Can you do that?"

"Er, uh, sure. I can do that," I said, unwilling to admit that I had rarely baptized anyone by immersion.

I arrived at the church that Sunday morning, and sure enough, there was the pastor standing on the front steps of the little church with a small boy.

"Jeremy, this is the bishop," the pastor said proudly. "It's an honor for you to be baptized by the bishop."

Young Jeremy looked me over and said only, "They tell me you don't do many of these. I'd feel better if we had a run-through beforehand."

"That was just what I was going to suggest," I said.

We went into the church's fellowship hall where the pastor showed me their newly purchased font, dressed up by a carpenter in the congregation, surrounded by pots of flowers. Jeremy said, "After you say the words, then you take my hand and lead me up these steps, and do you want me to take off my socks?"

"Er, uh, you can leave them on if you want," I said.

Well, we had a wonderful service that Sunday. I preached on baptism, the choir sang a baptismal anthem then the whole congregation recessed into the fellowship hall and gathered around the font. I went through the baptismal ritual. Then I asked Jeremy if he had anything to say to the congregation before his baptism.

"Yes, I do. I just want to say to all of you that I'm here today because of you. When my parents got divorced, I thought my world was over. But you stood by me. You told me the stories about Jesus. And I just want to say to you today thanks for what you did for me. I intend to make you proud as I'm going to try to live my life the way Jesus wants."

Though I'm now weeping profusely (Jeremy asked, as I led him up the steps into the pool, "Are you going to be OK?"), I baptized Jeremy and the church sang a great "Hallelujah!"

Baptism is God's word in water that saves. Not that the church necessarily says that we are saved by this ritual, but rather baptism gathers up all the meanings of Christian salvation and demonstrates those in word and water. The dying-rising dynamic that is signified in baptism is at the heart of salvation in Christ. The church promises that this has happened to you, is happening, will happen to you in your salvation. From this rich ritual we note a number of meanings about Christian salvation.

1. You can't save yourself. Baptism is a gift that is offered to you, not something done by you. So is your salvation.
2. Baptism is a sign that God works through the church to do for you what you cannot do for yourself, mainly to save you. This corporate, ecclesial gift they call salvation.
3. Baptism is a sign of a process that takes only a few minutes to do but the rest of your whole life to finish. That process is called salvation.
4. Baptism is a great comfort in life and in death because it reminds us that our relationship with God is something that is not utterly dependent upon us. When we call baptism a "sacrament" we are signifying that baptism is an act of God, a sign of God's self-giving, a public testimonial and confirmation of salvation.
5. In baptism there is an interplay between a gift offered and a gift received. There must be commitment, confession, response, and

transformation, but that doesn't all have to be done the day you are baptized. For some, baptism is the culmination of a long journey; for others, baptism is the beginning of a journey that will continue over a lifetime. As Luther said, every day we must bound out of bed and pray to God to continue the work begun in us in our baptism—namely dying and rising with Christ. Dying and rising with Christ is the dynamic at the heart of what we call "salvation."

So we would be justified, when asked "What is the meaning of salvation?" to reply simply, "Baptism."

LEARNING TO ENDURE THE LOVE OF JESUS

Pastoral care in the church is the sustained attempt to be with the people to whom this God has erotically turned, those who are being snared in the great dragnet of God's grace. Alas, much that passes for pastoral care is mere adjustment to the cultural status quo, adaptation through therapy or chemistry to governmentally sanctioned definitions of reality. True pastoral care in the name of Christ consists of encouragement to rebel against the illusory world that is produced by the modern state and its salvations and join God's revolution. I expect this is what Barth meant when he said that the mercy of God was much more demanding and difficult for humanity than the judgment of God. To be actively loved by God, really to know that God has decisively moved in with us and taken up our cause is desperately to need pastoral care to assist us in enduring such severe mercy. Most of the people in my church are fairly content and happy—until Jesus shows up. The trouble starts when they discover that salvation is inextricably linked to vocation. They experience awareness of their salvation not only as future blessing but also as present assignment.

We say in the Apostles' Creed that Christ "sitteth at the right hand of God the Father Almighty." It is a statement about rule, authority. But it's also a statement about the nature of God and what God is up to, not only in heaven but on earth. Seated there, at the right hand of the Father, it's hard for me to believe that Christ sits there in serene complacency. The Son who sits next to the Father is none other than the one who sought the sheep, intruded among the sinners, reached toward the unloved, the one who stooped to the wounded in the ditch. Now this one sits at the right hand of the Father, now in the power of the Holy Spirit works with the Father as embodiment of the Father's full *eros*.[5] This is great comfort.

Paul cries out in anguish, "Wretched man that I am! Who will rescue me from this body of death?" (Rom 7:24). This cry (uttered well *after* "conversion" on the Damascus road, I remind you) is quickly followed by the celebratory, "Thanks be to God through Jesus Christ our Lord!" I also note that Paul says, "I know in whom I have believed." Paul does not say, "I know what I believe," as if he believed in a system of ideas. Nor does he say, "I know that I believe," as if his belief were a free floating belief in belief. Paul's belief is personal trust in an engaging person—Jesus Christ.

To be loved by *this* person can be a challenge. The most controverted, tensive, and challenging thing about salvation in Jesus Christ is that it is *salvation in Jesus Christ*. If there is "no other name . . . by which we must be saved" (Acts 4:12), then those of us who know Jesus ought to understand better than anyone why many resist his rescue.

The popular movie *Crash* opens with a disgusting scene as an African American couple is stopped by two Caucasian policemen. One of the policemen, an obviously troubled middle-aged man, humiliates the couple by touching and probing the woman on the pretense that he is doing a search of her body, looking for weapons. It is a humiliating experience of racism and sexist evil.

The couple is enraged but feels helpless to do anything about it. Eventually, they separate, so angry is the woman that her husband stood by and did nothing, so humiliated and angry is the man that he was a helpless bystander as his beloved was humiliated by this racist cop.

Later in the movie, the same policeman comes upon a terrible accident. A car has flipped upside down. It is leaking gas. Trapped inside is the driver. The policeman moves into action, crawling inside the car. But when he climbs inside and the trapped driver sees him, she begins screaming, "No, no! Not you. Get away from me. Don't touch me!"

It is the same woman whom he earlier humiliated. She is obviously terrified to see him. Though she hangs upside down, and though gasoline is leaking all around her, she can't stand the thought of being near this man again, much less having him save her.

But the policeman acts as he has been trained. He attempts to calm her. He tells her that she is going to make it. He pulls out his knife and cuts her free, gently letting her down in the upside down car, eventually pulling her to safety just before the car explodes in flames.

As she is led away by others, she looks over her shoulder and sees that the cop, the man who had so terribly wronged her now is the one responsible for saving her life. She must live as one who has been saved, indebted to a man whom she hates. Her savior is the perpetrator of a terrible, sinful act. It is all very complicated.

Salvation is complicated because of the complicated trinitarian God who saves. We are saved by the one whom we despise. Unlike in *Crash*, we are saved not by the one who abused us, but the one whom we abused. The one whom we crucified in a desperate attempt to be left alone becomes our savior who refuses to be God without us. And in being saved we are also indebted, enlisted, and bound in discipleship to the one who has suffered because of us and yet suffered for us in order to save us. Our salvation by the crucified Christ thus presses upon us heavy responsibility to live with the risen Christ. His salvation makes our lives more complex than if we had not been reached to and embraced by him. Even now God is searching through the large collection of divine fishhooks for just the right lure to catch you in order to embrace you in order eternally to enjoy you.

All we know of salvation, our final end, our ultimate hope, is Jesus Christ who keeps trying zealously to *eros* us, *sōzō* completely, rescue us, heal us, perfectly to have us be all that he intends. Salvation is, therefore, also the name for the adventure of being the objects of the love of a God who is Father, Son, and Holy Spirit *pro nobis*. Charles Wesley's hymns are about as sensuous as most of us Methodists get. Wesley knew that to be loved by God is to be changed in the embrace. As usual, Wesley says it better than I:

> Finish, then, thy new creation;
> pure and spotless let us be.
> Let us see thy great salvation
> perfectly restored in thee:
> changed from glory into glory,
> till in heaven we take our place,
> till we cast our crowns before thee,
> lost in wonder, love, and praise.[6]

CHAPTER THREE

DIVINE ABUNDANCE

I have a friend, a lawyer, who is something of a theologian. He finds it a salubrious spiritual exercise to sit in an airport waiting lounge and to focus on people—as they walk by or sit across from him—and ask, "Did Jesus Christ die for this person?"

He attempts to expand his gaze, focusing on the oddest person in the lounge and ask, "Jesus Christ died for *him?*"

He explains, "It's my little discipline to see just how much I can swallow about Jesus Christ without choking."

As we have said, all we know about our true present situation and our eternal destiny is what has been revealed to us in the life and teachings of Jesus Christ—our knowledge of salvation is not tied to human questing or yearning. I need to say that because Freud has convinced many modern people that our sense of God is only a projection of our wishes and desires. (The modern world loved these reductive, "it is only" statements.) We wish that we had eternality so we project a being ("God") who gives us what we want. "God" has no reality other than as a projection of our desires.

As we discovered after being assaulted by the parables of Jesus, salvation is not what we asked for. If we were merely projecting an eternal destiny for ourselves, we could have projected a more benign future than the one that meets us in Jesus! As Calvin said, the human mind is a permanent factory for idols that we find more agreeable than the Trinity.

The question "Is there salvation and who is it for?" is an inquiry into the identity of God. Who saves? It is not a matter of what we think we need or deserve in order to give our lives some measure of sustainability and permanence. Salvation requires an inquiry into what God wants. Salvation is the peculiar "yes" that is spoken to us, spoken even before we ask, in Jesus Christ. Salvation is God's projection of God's desires upon us.

We know this only on the basis of the stories of Jesus. A farmer goes forth to sow seed and—carefully, meticulously—prepares the ground,

removing all rocks and weeds, sowing one seed six inches from another?
No. The farmer, without preparation, begins slinging seed. A dragnet is
hauled into the boat full of creatures both good and bad. Should the catch
be sorted, separating the good from the bad? No. The Master is more impressed with the size of the haul than with the quality of the harvest. One
day, not today, it will all be sorted.

A field is planted with good seed. But a perverse enemy sows weeds in
the field. Should we cull the wheat from the weeds? No. The Master says
that someday he will judge good from bad, but we are not to bother ourselves with such sorting today. The Master seems to be more into careless
sowing, miraculous growing, and reckless harvesting than in taxonomy of
the good from the bad, the worthwhile from the worthless, the saved from
the damned.

"Which one of you?" to paraphrase Jesus' questions in Luke 15, "having lost one sheep will not leave the ninety-nine sheep to fend for themselves in the wilderness and beat the bushes until you find the one lost
sheep? Which one of you will not put that sheep on your shoulders like a
lost child and say to your friends, 'Come party with me'? Which one of
you would not do that?"

"Which of you women," Jesus continues, "if you lose a quarter will not
rip up the carpet and strip the house bare and when you have found your
lost coin run into the street and call to your neighbors, 'Come party with
me, I found my quarter!' Which one of you would not do that?"

And which of you fathers, having two sons, the younger of whom
leaves home, blows all your money, comes dragging back home in rags, will
not throw the biggest bash this town has ever seen, singing, "This son of
mine was dead but is now alive!" Which one of you would not do that?

And which of you, journeying down the Jericho Road, upon seeing a
perfect stranger lying in the ditch half dead, bleeding, would not risk your
life, put the injured man in the backseat of your Jaguar, take him to the
hospital, spend every dime you have on his recovery, and more. Which of
you would not do that?

The answer is that *none of us* would behave in this unseemly, reckless,
and extravagant way. These are not stories about us. These are God's stories—God the searching shepherd, the careless farmer, the undiscerning
fisherman, the reckless woman, the extravagant father, the prodigal Samaritan. Jesus thus reveals a God who is no discrete minimalist. Abundance
is in the nature of this God. So when Jesus, confronted by the hunger of
the multitudes (Mark 8), took what his disciples had and blessed it, there

was not only enough to satisfy the hungry ones but also a surplus, more than enough. Jesus demonstrates a surfeit that is at the heart of all God-given reality.

There is a pervasive nihilism at the heart of modernity, a sense of scarcity. We are on our own, making our way in a world of want as best we can with insufficient information and not enough love. Freud, who did much to form the modern mind, spoke of "obscure, unfeeling, and unloving powers"[1] that determine our fate, reviving the early Greek view that we are, in Homer's words, mere "toys of the gods." If there are gods in the heaven above, they do not reveal themselves to us and have no benevolent intent for us here on earth below. This is a story that captivates modernity.

A Christian is someone who looks upon the world, the passing scene of current events, the sweep of history, her own life, and believes that there is, despite our first impressions of nothing, not just something but Someone. There is a discernible pattern. We look, with non-Christians, at the same events, the same history, and yet we see a distinctive movement in a particular direction, a surfeit of meaning. Salvation is the story, the whole story, from beginning to end, the discernible shape of the narrative that is being told by God, not just the end of the story. Christians become protagonists in God's story. This is what it means to be saved.

In these Bible stories a central character emerges. Unfortunately, well-meaning commentators have placed titles on the stories, subheadings in your Bible like, "The Prodigal Son," or the "Laborers in the Vineyard." Yet in reading the stories, we are surprised to find that all the stories are about God. They render an agent, a personality so that they ought to be called, "The Prodigal Father," or the "Ridiculously Gracious Farmer." Most of us have been conditioned to listen to Scripture anthropologically rather than theologically, asking, "How is this story about me?" Therefore, we need a general interpretive principle for reading the Bible: Scripture always and everywhere speaks primarily about God, and only secondarily, and then only derivatively, about us.

God gets the story started, and God sustains the story, intervening from time to time, making a way when there is no way, nudging forward, despite twists and turns, subplots and diversions, holding to the overall intent of the story, calling in a surprising cast of actors, all the while remaining the author and the chief actor in the story. The name of the story is *salvation*.

At the end of one of his most demanding, exacting sermons, requiring that his disciples turn the other cheek, refuse to divorce and remarry, carry others' burdens not just one mile but two, and to pray for their enemies

(Matthew 5), Jesus extravagantly demands that they be "perfect . . . as your heavenly Father is perfect" (v. 48). But then he characterizes the Father's perfection as one who "makes his sun rise on the evil and on the good, and sends rain on the righteous and on the unrighteous" (v. 45). It is of our nature to make careful distinctions, to draw accurate lines between people, to conceive of reality as characterized by scarcity and insufficiency. But it is of the nature of this God to blur our proper divisions by indiscriminately, profusely sending rain and sun upon all without distinction.

In the Gospel of Luke, the Baptist who prepares the way for Christ joyfully announces, "all flesh shall see the salvation of God" (Luke 3:6). Did John really mean "all" are to see "the salvation of God"? That is the question to which we now turn in our exploration of salvation in Jesus Christ.

ALL?

On a late September Sunday in 1957, the great theologian Karl Barth once again preached to the prisoners in the Basel jail. The title for his sermon was simply, "All!" His one verse text: "For God has imprisoned all in disobedience so that he may be merciful to all" (Rom 11:32).[2] Barth told the prisoners that here was a lofty mountain "which we cannot climb, in our thoughts or in a sermon," a mountain "from which we can only climb down." Barth focuses first on the second phrase of the text—"God has mercy on us. He says 'yes' to us, he wills to be on our side, to be our God against all odds." Note that Barth's sermon begins with focus upon what God has done and now does. In my experience, this homiletical approach is rare among today's preachers. The homiletical mode in modernity is to begin with humanity—who we are and what we must do. Then, after confidently asserting my anthropological observations, I make a few concluding, halting theological claims about how helpful God can be in achieving who we want to be and what we want to do. Barth begins with God, beginning with what we know of God from God's revelation, believing that we really don't know who we are until we know who God is and what God has created us for.

Then Barth notes that this "all" is without qualification—Gentiles, atheists, believers, nonbelievers, those who have been formally incarcerated, and those who sit in judgment upon them—"all."

Barth confesses that sometimes he is guilty of wishing that this "all" did not include, "this fellow-creature beside me, in front of me or behind, whom I don't like." Then he admits to the intention of his sermon: "The one great sin from which we shall try to escape this morning is to exclude anyone from the 'yes' of God's mercy." All are prisoners; all are shown mercy.

Barth gives thanks that he is preaching "in a house where there are so many closed doors," where he doesn't have to expend much homiletical effort explaining the word "prisoner." He then reminds the inmates that the text says that "all" are prisoners—some enslaved by socialist utopian dreams, others imprisoned by illness or the deprivations "of the so-called 'free world,' not to mention death." Barth implies that the prisoners have an advantage in understanding the Scripture since their imprisonment is undeniable, unlike the faithful at First Church Basel.

Disobedience to God is our primary enslavement, says Barth. We have relegated God to the "man upstairs" so we can "go our own ways" downstairs. Sometimes our disobedience becomes downright religious as we attempt "an impossible ascent" up the mountain as "foolish mountainclimbers" who arrogantly refuse to let God descend to us as we piously, stupidly attempt to ascend to God through our rituals, churches, beliefs, and deeds. Whereas I've heard people define religion as something that all people do to get up the mountain to God, Barth defines religion as a means God uses to descend down the mountain to us.

The preacher is careful to include himself in this "all"—"each and all, are prisoners of disobedience." All. "He who knows Jesus knows this," says Barth. It's hard for us to know the depth and scope of our disobedience until Jesus Christ makes our sin painfully clear to us. (Barth implies here that confrontation with a merciful God precedes confrontation with our disobedience.) In Jesus, God shows God's glory—God is merciful to the disobedient. Barth ends his sermon by asserting, "Joy is born when you renounce any attempt to be something more than one among all those whom God has made prisoners of disobedience, that he may have mercy on all." There is great joy in knowing that one's greatest claim upon God is that "I'm disobedient" because we now know a God who has mercy only for the disobedient.

All the perpetrators of disobedience; all the recipients of mercy. "This salvation of God" (Acts 28:28) is the great mystery of a God who refuses to be God alone. All sin; God's mercy is actively available for all sinners.

One of the more bizarre aspects of Richard Dawkins's *The God Delusion*[3] is Dawkins' claim that religions like Christianity foster exclusion and an insider and outsider mentality. Professor Dawkins appears not to have read that Jesus was criticized consistently as one who "welcomes sinners and eats with them" (Luke 15:2). A search of the embracing little word *all* in the New Testament reveals that inclusion was in the nature of Jesus. When Jesus miraculously provides bread in the wilderness, not just his followers but "all . . . ate and were filled" (Matt 15:37). In the parable of the great banquet, after a failed attempt to invite close friends and cronies, the lord of the banquet "gathered all whom they found, both good and bad" (Matt 22:10). Jesus predicts that "all who exalt themselves will be humbled, and all who humble themselves will be exalted" (Matt 23:12). His message is "a testimony to all the nations" (Matt 24:14). In the climactic scene in the temple Jesus declares that the temple is not just for Israel but is "a house of prayer for all the nations" (Mark 11:17). He promises that when he is lifted upon the cross, "I . . . will draw all people to myself" (John 12:32). He is the "true light, which enlightens everyone" (John 1:9). He calls to himself "all you that are weary and are carrying heavy burdens" (Matt 11:28). The psalmist even exclaims that God saves not only all people but even all animals (Ps 36:6)!

When I stand and read the Christmas Epistle, I announce before the congregation that the Incarnation is not just for those who are here on other Sundays but even for those who show up just on Christmas—"For the grace of God has appeared, bringing salvation to all" (Titus 2:11).

In my classes at the university, it was my custom to grade more or less "on the curve." After all, I can't give A's to everyone. So to avoid grade inflation I was careful to give A's only to some, those in the upper 20 percent. God, Jesus says, is not like that.

Here is a tiny sect in a forlorn corner of the empire, centered upon devotion to a Jew, a criminal who was tortured to death by the authorities, a little fringe group of extremists holding on by their fingernails. They had managed to establish a few pitiful congregations here and there in the hinterland. Though Jesus had once called them the "light of the world" (Matt 5:14), their light seemed fragile and dim, no real competitor with the brilliance of the Empire. Yet when they spoke of *salvation* they told of an event no less cosmic and world shattering than the end and the beginning of all things. They felt commanded to proclaim this salvation to the ends of the earth (Acts 1:8), to enlist disciples from *all* nations, both Israel and Rome, without distinction (Matt 28:19). All.

Previously they had made careful, religious distinctions between Gentile and Jew, male and female, now they claimed all such distinctions were destroyed in the inclusive embrace of Christ. Though they appear to have had next to nothing by way of security or property, Paul told the ragtag crowd of Christ followers at Corinth, "the world or life or death or the present or the future—all belong to you, and you belong to Christ, and Christ belongs to God" (1 Cor 3:22-23). There was a sort of reckless extravagance in their behavior. They took everything they had and piled it all together to be used for the care of all (Acts 4:32). They bragged about having no personal property or possessions, now having "all things in common." All.

On Pentecost, Jews from every nation in the world gathered (Acts 2). In a miraculous descent of the Holy Spirit, this little sect became multilingual, universal. The church was thrust everywhere, showing up all over. Not twenty years after their Savior had been humiliatingly crucified by the authorities, Paul told them that they would judge the world and the angels (1 Cor 6:2-3). They were God's major means of reconciling the world (Rom 11:15; 2 Cor 5:19). God's whole plan for all the world was being revealed through them (Eph 3:9-10). "This was not done in a corner" (Acts 26:26), Paul stood up and preached to King Agrippa. "This salvation of God" was huge, cosmic (Acts 28:28). All.

The basis for these effusive claims about God's salvation was something that had happened to them. Nobody is more extravagant than Paul in his sweeping declaration of what has actually occurred in our salvation. No longer jerked around by "the elemental spirits of the world" (Gal 4:3, 9), the otherwise intimidating "powers" (Rom 8:38; cf. 1 Cor 2:6-10), they stood up and spoke up, now free from sin and death (1 Cor 15:54-57). They spoke not about an opinion that they shared, a new theory they had devised; they spoke of a series of events (they often said they were being saved [Rom 1:16; 10:10; Eph 2:5-8]) that had happened to them, something even now happening. "For freedom Christ has set us free," (Gal 5:1) Paul preached on his way to jail. Note that he spoke in the past tense, claiming a gift presently received rather than only a future expectation.

As a preacher I note that a principal evidence put forth by early Christians as proof of their salvation was their experience of bold, free speech (*parrhēsia,* in Acts 2:29; 4:13, 29). The same Peter who couldn't find his tongue to tell about Jesus when confronted by the little serving girl in the courtyard at midnight (Matt 26:69-75), after the Resurrection, stands up and delivers the gospel with boldness (Acts 2:14-47).

You know how people fear public speaking. To speak in favor of a criminal who died on a cross must have been even more fearful. Yet they preached. To the experience of homiletical boldness, the disciples added testimony to "peace" (Rom 5:1; 14:17), "joy" even amid suffering (1 Thess 3:6-9; Heb 12:1-3), as well as "faith, hope, and love" (1 Cor 13:13; 1 Thess 1:2-3). In short, they claimed many of the gifts and dispensations that Israel had come to expect in the messianic age as their own. Get it? The Christians believed that they were the first fruits of God's promised salvation of Israel, only in a form that was wider, more extravagant and reckless than even Israel had imagined.

Christian salvation is thus inextricably linked to the story of Israel's salvation. "All Israel will be saved," says Paul (Rom 11:26), repeating what Israel had always believed. But now Paul expands "all" to include even Gentiles. It is not that Christian salvation supersedes Israel's salvation but rather that Israel's story could now be a story for others as well. We Gentiles had, in an amazing act of God, been engrafted into the promises of God to Israel. What Israel expected from their beloved Torah, Jewish and Gentile Christians in the first centuries after Jesus' death and resurrection claimed to have experienced in Jesus. Paul makes the astounding claim that Jesus Christ saves people that nobody thought could be saved.

> O the depth of the riches and wisdom and knowledge of God! How unsearchable are his judgments and how inscrutable his ways!
> "For who has known the mind of the Lord?
> Or who has been his counselor?"
> "Or who has given a gift to him to receive a gift in return?"
> For from him and through him and to him are all things. To him be glory for ever. Amen. (Rom 11:33-36)

And they were careful to speak of this unmerited gift, not as future hope but as present experience, not as rescue from a negative situation but rather as a gift of a positive new life here, now. Paul asserts in Romans that "now" God's righteousness is revealed (3:21), "now" they are made into righteousness (5:9), "now" they are reconciled to God (5:11), "now" there is no condemnation by the law (8:1). Right now they had "power" (Rom 1:16) not of their own devising. Now there were salvific "signs and wonders" (Acts 4:30; 5:12; Rom 15:19) that included miraculous healings, speaking in tongues, and above all proclamation of the good news (2 Cor 4:7; 1 Thess 1:5). "See . . . *now* is the day of *salvation*" (2 Cor 6:2, italics mine).

They were clear that this power, these contemporary gifts "for us and for our salvation" were not of their own devising (Rom 1:4; 16:25; 1 Cor 1:24). Forgiveness of sin, setting right things between us and God is a work of God. "The wages of sin is death, but the free gift of God is eternal life in Christ Jesus our Lord" (Rom 6:23). In a day when Jesus is often depicted as our very dear personal friend, as a thoughtful moral teacher, what's left after the search for the historical Jesus has rummaged about in the past, the Creed's cosmic assertion that Jesus "came down from heaven . . . for our salvation" is invigorating. Here is a God who is not only love but is love in action, love on the move toward us. "No one has ascended into heaven except the one who descended from heaven, the Son of Man" (John 3:13).

> Though he was in the form of God, [he] did not regard equality with God
> as something to be exploited, but emptied himself, taking the form of a
> slave, being born in human likeness. (Phil 2:6-7)

After hearing an exponent of so-called progressive Christianity expound breathlessly on his discovery of Jesus as a proto-revolutionary wisdom sage, a young woman next to me asked quietly, "Why bother?"

Why indeed? Our minimalist Christology issues forth a flaccid salvation—a "god" who doesn't really do anything except to encourage basically good, progressive people who don't need anything done for them anyway. Educated, Western, upper-middle-class people don't need much of a savior, so we tend to honor the god who cares about us but never acts for us, who feels a certain vague affection for us but never gets around to doing anything for us, a god certainly not reckless enough to die for us. In this cultural context, salvation is reduced to recovery, or a sense of meaning in life, or a positive self-attitude. Why bother?

And don't you find it rather sad that some other segments of contemporary Christianity so stress the power of sin and evil that they detract from the power of God's salvation? We are such great, impressive sinners that even God can't help us. Theodicy (justification of the ways of God to humanity) is all the rage in a church that has forgotten how to worship a God who saves. *Left Behind* books speak of salvation as some future state of bliss when God will at last make good on God's postponed promises by delivering just a precious few righteous from the mass of the sinful rabble in this sin-dominated world. Salvation thus conceived is exclusively a future hope rather than a present reality. The title of Hal Lindsey's (now justly forgotten) book *Satan Is Alive and Well on Planet Earth*[4] implies that not much happened on the cross for us and our salvation. Satan trumped Jesus. Paul got it wrong after all. Present experience of the power of sin, evil, and death overwhelms present enjoyment of God's great victory in Christ. For contemporary culture, 9/11 is the new world order. "Help, I've fallen down and can't get up!" is our motto. Cosmic salvation is rendered into something personal and subjective. The world is going to hell, but we can still feel saved if we try. Our expectation of postponed future bliss is impotent to bring present transformation. We are thus in danger of proclaiming "this salvation of God" as true but living as if it were not.

WHO IS SAVED?

If we think about salvation at all, it is curious, and a bit sad, how we tend to move from claims that "Jesus saves" immediately to the question, "*Who* is saved?" First, candor. We are limited in our ability to answer that question because we are inquiring into a matter that is God's self-assigned task rather than ours. Salvation names what God in Christ Jesus has done, is doing, and will do with us. As Jesus puts it, "You did not choose me but I chose you" (John 15:16). In saying "salvation," we are talking about something that only God can do. Nothing about us contributes to our salvation. John Wesley would have me add, salvation is not simply about heaven, the afterlife after we die. Salvation is here, now, whenever we get caught up in the divine life. But who is saved?

The Revelation to John pulls back the curtain of eternity and gives us a glimpse of salvation completed:

> Then I looked, and I heard the voice of many angels surrounding the throne and the living creatures and the elders; they numbered myriads of myriads and thousands of thousands, singing with full voice,
>   "Worthy is the Lamb that was slaughtered
>   to receive power and wealth and wisdom and might
>   and honor and glory and blessing!"
> Then I heard every creature in heaven and on earth and under the earth and in the sea, and all that is in them, singing,
>   "To the one seated on the throne and to the Lamb
>   be blessing and honor and glory and might
>   forever and ever!" (Rev 5:11-13)

One might think that the Revelation—addressed to a persecuted and struggling church—would stress the fortunate few rescued and safe before the Lamb's throne. Although Revelation is not above such limiting judgments, here Revelation's stress is upon the "myriads of myriads and thousands of thousands." A huge crowd is gathered before the throne, a massive, constantly processing choir made up not only of myriads of people, but even "of every creature in heaven and on earth and under the earth and in the sea."

Salvation is not only for humans but even for the whales? Behold: a fallen, silenced Creation healed. Our post-Genesis 1–2 situation has been fixed. The creatures are singing. Creation and redemption are together. Revelation 5 leads us to suppose that this life in a fallen world is but a long choir rehearsal. One day, there before the throne, we shall take our places among the myriads of myriads, with the humpback whales and bullfinches, the wolves and the lemurs, with those whom we have loved (and, presumably, with the myriads whom we have despised), all singing with one voice, "Blessing and honor and glory and might to the Lamb!"

It's quite a sweeping, embracing heavenly performance. Is the poetry true? Might we expect myriads of myriads? Is the Bible once again engaging in hyperbole? All?

In his *Crossing the Threshold of Hope*, Pope John Paul II wrote that, although there sure is a hell, the Church has never said for sure who, if anyone, is in hell.[5] We do not even know, the Pope says, whether Judas Iscariot is in hell. If we can't say for sure that Judas is in hell, why not everybody? Or perhaps more the point, if I have some reason to believe that *I'm* not in hell, then why not believe that hell might be empty?

Richard Neuhaus criticizes a relatively recent form of Christian thought that, says Neuhaus, trivializes the question by its individualistic, "Am *I* saved?" The sweeping, cosmic claims that were celebrated in the Revelation to John are reduced to a personal preoccupation: am *I* going to heaven?

To be honest, I don't hear many too troubled with, "Am I saved?" Luther's struggle—where can I find a loving God?—is more often today, I'm certain that God loves me, but could the God who loves me even love *you*? Recently, in a conversation on this subject, I noted that no one asked, "How could Jesus die for a sinner like me?" but rather, "Do you think that Hitler will go to heaven?"

Although the question of your individual, eternal destiny is important, Paul says that it is tied to a consideration of the whole of God's purpose for Creation. First Timothy declares that God "desires everyone to be saved and to come to the knowledge of the truth" (1 Tim 2:4). Considering the incredible lengths to which God went to retrieve us, in the life, death, and resurrection of Christ, is it possible that God's desire will be thwarted? Neuhaus asks, if God is severely limited in God's attainment of God's desires, can we call the one so limited "God"? It's one thing for God's purposes to be stymied by our sin in the present moment, but will

God never ever get what God wants? I would be the last to claim that everything that is happening right now is "God's will," but will God's purposes for humanity be forever contested? John 3:16, the first scripture I was made to memorize as a child, says, "God so loved the world that he gave his only Son." Has God's love of the world been reduced by the world to apply to only some of the world? Was the incredible sacrifice of Christ on the cross truly, universally effective for all or only conditionally effective for a few?

You know how, through the ark of Noah, God rescued a righteous remnant, allowing the many to perish. But do you know the full implications of the story told by 1 Timothy, suggesting that God's plan is now more bold than to rescue a religious elite (that is, everyone in this room) from an otherwise botched creation? No one is more convincing than Paul in proclaiming that God's present desire is restoration of all things in Christ:

> In him we have redemption through his blood, the forgiveness of our trespasses, according to the riches of his grace that he lavished on us . . . he has made known to us . . . to gather up all things in him, things in heaven and things on earth. (Eph 1:7-10)

You can't miss that *to gather up all things in him*. Paul has poetically sailed beyond the merely personal, "Jesus died for my sins," or "I know that I will be in heaven." God's desire, in Jesus Christ, is akin to God's cosmic desire in Genesis 1 and 2. God is still busy bringing worlds into being that were not. The restless Creator became the relentless Redeemer. The Redeemer is the same fabricator of the chaos whom we met as Creator. The work of the cosmic Christ is cosmic salvation.

Picture Paul preaching this bodacious, universal claim to a little group of Christians huddled together at their house church in Colossae:

> He is the image of the invisible God, the firstborn of all creation; for in him all things in heaven and on earth were created, things visible and invisible, whether thrones or dominions or rulers or powers—all things have been created through him and for him . . . in him all things hold together. . . . For in him all the fullness of God was pleased to dwell, and through him God was pleased to reconcile to himself all things, whether on earth or in heaven, by making peace through the blood of his cross. (Col 1:15-20)

To unite all things in him. To reconcile all to himself. All. Just when we settle in—just me and my friends who are saved—here comes Jesus proclaiming, "I have other sheep that do not belong to this fold. I must bring them also" (John 10:16).

Is the hope of universal restoration, the hope that all people will be saved—that hell will not be eternal and that God will eventually be "all in all" (1 Cor 15:28)—a legitimate Christian hope? The Acts of the Apostles recounts Peter's preaching of a "universal restoration" [*apokatastasis*] that "God announced long ago through his holy prophets" (Acts 3:21). The hope of universal restoration, *apokatastasis* is an idea that has rarely been regarded as fully orthodox; still this hope has rarely been actively opposed by the church, perhaps because there is enough biblical material to keep the matter open to argument. The great fourth-century Cappadocian Gregory of Nyssa taught that the Resurrection will finally restore human beings to their original state before the Fall. This life, in this world, is a long journey in which the *imago dei* stamped upon us at Creation, the image of God that has been defaced due to our sin, is gradually more fully realized and eventually completely reconstituted. "For God all things are possible" (Mark 10:27). The Augustinian-Lutheran-Calvinist counterview—some are saved and some are damned—has tended to prevail. The human race is divided by God into two distinct groups: the elect, who have received God's mercy, and the rejected, who have received God's judgment.

FOR WHAT MIGHT WE HOPE?

Karl Barth revived the question of whether we can hope, whether we should hope, that in the end all will be saved. Let me quickly sketch Barth's take on salvation. Barth loved the phrase "Jesus is Victor!" even more than the biblical "Jesus is Lord." Jesus is not just love but active, resourceful, victorious love that has defeated the principalities and powers, stripped them of their pretense, and forever secured all creation as his territory. Although many (most?) of the human beneficiaries of Christ's saving, victorious work may be oblivious to Christ's triumph, that doesn't change the fact. God's Genesis assault upon chaos was brought to glorious fulfillment in Jesus' victory on Golgotha. The providential grace of God that many experience in their day-to-day lives is the same as the redeeming grace of God that confronts us and saves us in the cross of Christ. Both divine actions (creation and redemption) have the same divine purpose—to draw all things unto God.

Politically, this means that Jesus' victory has left us with only one realm—the kingdom of God. Other principalities, whether they be those of United States, the United Kingdom, or Satan, exist now only in our minds, in our constrained imaginations, as mere shadows of their former selves. Barth says that Satan's realm is a "shadow kingdom," a pseudo-kingdom that is no longer a significant threat to anybody now that Jesus Christ rules. "This kingdom is behind us and all [people]. We and all [people] are released from . . . this prison"[6] The world has been exorcised. That's one reason why at baptism, we ask candidates for a renunciation of participation in the realm of evil and wickedness. Baptism is a sort of transfer of citizenship. Baptism into Christ saves (1 Pet 3:21).

Barth stresses that even those who neither know nor acknowledge this, even those who actively resist this change in citizenship, still find themselves living in this realm, "claimed and absorbed by his act of obedience."[7] Because Jesus Christ's reign is an accomplished fact, it can never be forever external to them because eventually all of us succumb to the facts of life. The church preaches this reality and invites people who haven't heard the news to hear the news and to go ahead now and live in light of the facts—Jesus Christ is Lord.

Barth says, "There is no one who does not participate in him in this turning to God. There is no one who is not . . . engaged in this turning. There is no one who is not raised and exalted with him to true humanity. 'Jesus Christ lives, and I with him.'"[8] Salvation is not so much a commentary on who decides for Christ ("Since I gave my life to Jesus") as it is a celebration of those for whom Christ has decided (You don't so much give your life to Christ as Christ takes it.). Barth says that it is important for the church to admit that this salvation of God "is for each and every human being, and not merely for the people of God."[9]

Of course there are people who resist or deny this cosmic, political claim about sovereignty. But how much credence ought we to give to human resistance and denial? If Jesus Christ died on the cross to defeat human sin, Barth is reluctant to concede much continuing power to human sin, which is why Barth was charged by many as guilty of "universalism." Barth denied the charge, saying that he was willing to concede that self-damnation might be an "impossible possibility" but to assert "universal salvation" would do "violence to the New Testament."[10]

What Barth denied in the idea of *apokatastasis* was to make universal salvation inevitable. To in any way imply that God *must* save would be to make our salvation a law or a general principle and to do so would be to limit the freedom and sovereignty of God.

To the person who doggedly, persistently denies the lordship of Christ and turns away from the open hand of salvation, "God does not owe eternal patience and . . . deliverance" says Barth.[11] But if there are limits upon the love and patience of God, or if there are no limits to the love and patience of God, those matters are in God's hands, not ours. Though we must not expect certitude in these matters, says Barth, we can still "hope." Salvation, whether of all or a few, must always be an "article of hope,"[12] because it is a matter in the hands of a sovereign God. "That . . . you may know . . . the hope to which he has called you . . . God put this power to work in Christ. . . . And he has put all things under his feet . . . the fullness of him who fills all in all" (Eph 1:18-23). Such hope is not wishful thinking but rather engendered in us by scripture such as Romans 12:29 on the irrevocable gifts of God and 2 Timothy 2:13 on the desire of God.

Barth puts into perspective the much-praised Reformation principle of "justification by faith." "Faith"—our response to God—is not in itself saving. Roman Catholics have spoken of our faith as animated by love whereas Protestants stress that faith must be exclusively initiated and constantly sustained by its object, Christ. Barth reminds us that the quality or quantity of our love or our believing is not that which saves. Faith is not that which is undertaken by us but rather that which we undergo when the fact of Christ's work floods in upon us with undeniable force. Faith is a gift, pure grace, which is to say that it is miraculous.

Barth wants to eliminate any sense that God's love for us is somehow conditional upon or determined by us. Though the Reformers affirmed salvation by God's grace alone, many of their heirs came to speak of salvation as a result of something we did, thought, or felt: "If you repent and believe, then you will be saved. If not, you will not be saved." We like that message because we live in a culture in which our subjectivity and our actions tend to be everything.

Barth's view of salvation is strongly "objective"—our feelings and response have little to do with it. Barth means to say, in effect, Jesus Christ has accomplished your salvation. This is an undeniable, ultimately irresistible fact. Now live in the light of the fact—repent and believe the good news. We need not strive to be included in salvation; in Jesus Christ all are included as the gift of the miraculous love of God in Christ. By stressing this objective, accomplished quality of salvation, Barth hopes to defeat any modernist notion that salvation is just another personal preference, something that human beings fabricate.

For humans to attempt to deny the work of Christ (and Barth seems unwilling to give such denial more than the status of an attempt) is a nonsensical, irrational act. But of course we do stupid things all the time. It is risky to swim against the tide of divine grace, but we often try. To attempt to will something that is against the will of God is to put one's puny little choices and pitiful little will against the desires of God, which is stupid. Whether a rebellious, intransigent, stupid human resistance to God's desires can go on forever, in the light of Barth's strong emphasis of the victorious grace of God, is dubious. Still, we commit so many dubious, self-destructive acts now, in this life, in this world, who can say for sure that we may not continue into whatever future we are given?

Reformer John Calvin had an equally high regard for the work of Christ, yet Calvin reflected on the mystery of human rejection by teaching a limited view of election—Christ elects for redemption some but not all—"double predestination." Barth rejects this and thereby moves closer to Wesley and Luther in having faith in the ultimate triumph of the grace of God. God's grace is everything and is for everyone, even if everyone is (oddly) not for grace. For instance, in commenting on Acts 10:34-35, Wesley says that God "does not confine His love to one nation" but "willeth all men should be saved."[13]

Calvin wondered why God might include some and exclude others. Barth wondered why this God would risk all, suffer and die, for all, not just a select, fortunate few. Barth is also mystified by why many, not just a few, seem to deny or reject such divine love. Still Barth maintains that even those who do not realize that they are caught up in the sweep of God's grace, even those who actively resist such grace, are still objects of grace despite their stupid contumacy.

Barth creatively taught a sort of predestination: from the beginning, God rejects sin, but Jesus Christ is the only one who is predestined for rejection. On the cross, Jesus cried out as abandoned and godforsaken. Barth said that Jesus was rejected by God on the cross and, when he was rejected, he was rejected in behalf of all. The just wrath of God against sin, the wages of which is death, has come down upon God's beloved Son, God's own self. Because God's own Son has been rejected by God, then welcomed back by the Father in the Resurrection, no human beings are rejected.

Scripture teaches that Jesus was elected by God from the foundation of the world to be the Savior of the world. Calvin's Reformed doctrine teaches what appears to be said in Ephesians 1:3-6—God elects some to be

God's children before the foundation of the world. Yet even in Calvin's teaching on election—God consigns some to salvation, some to perdition—there is a claim that the true church, the elect, is always "invisible." By this Calvin does not mean that the church can't be seen but rather that God's choices are sovereign, and so it has not been given to us fully to see whom God has elected for what future. According to Calvin, there is no justification for identifying anyone, including yourself, as numbered among either the saved or the reprobate. Their names and number are known only to God. We are charged to live on the basis of what we know of the love and mercy of God, certain that our eternal status is not based on who we are or what we do but rather upon God's sovereign election.

For now, we just don't know. But we are free to live on the basis of what God has graciously revealed to us. Many do not know that Jesus Christ is savior of the world and that he is determined to be their savior. The promise of Isaiah is that one day an effusively revealing God shall render a world in which "the earth will be full of the knowledge of the LORD as the waters cover the sea" (Isa 11:9). That's a lot of theology, spread far and wide.

For now, the church's task is to proclaim, in word and deed, the grand fact of our salvation. "But you are a chosen race, a royal priesthood, a holy nation, God's own people, in order that you may proclaim the mighty acts of him who called you out of darkness into his marvelous light" (1 Pet 2:9). The benefits of Jesus' atoning work extend to all, though sadly, not all know the facts; therefore, we are called to preach the "mighty acts of him who called you out of darkness into his marvelous light."

Although Barth admitted that we don't *know* all will be saved, he had no doubt that we should *desire* that all be saved, for that is what God desires, and it is axiomatic that we should want what God wants. This is close to what John Wesley taught, and the reason why early on we Wesleyans were accused of being "universalists."[14] Wesley taught universal redemption, complete atonement for all through the work of Christ on the cross.[15] Yet Wesley also knew that some tragically refuse this gift. So Wesley taught that whereas there is, in Christ, universal atonement, there may not be our universal salvation. It may be the case that although salvation is offered to all, available for all, it may not be guaranteed for all. Who knows how many of our stupid choices God will allow to shape our eternal destiny? God's grace is enabling rather than coercive. God has graciously left us room for some degree of synergy, some degree of responsible exchange in this matter of our relationship with God.

Still, God won't let the question of complete restoration end with that. The God of Scripture has this wonderful way of showing up just as we thought the story was ending, and by showing up, continuing the story, giving the story a more interesting ending than the drama would have had, had there not been a God who loves to raise the dead. A large degree of optimism is warranted by the biblical evidence.

A farmer needs workers for his vineyard (Matthew 20). So he arises early, goes out and finds some willing workers to harvest his grapes, agreeing with them on the usual daily wage. An invitation has been offered and accepted. End of story.

But as is so often with Jesus, it isn't the end of the story. Midmorning we are surprised to find the farmer back downtown, hiring more workers for his vineyard, agreeing to pay them "what's right." At noon, mid-afternoon, *one hour before quitting time*, the farmer is out wheeling and dealing, seemingly unable to rest until everyone in town is working in his vineyard. And Jesus says, God's kingdom is like that.

Peter, the premier disciple, in the Upper Room, at the end, promises, "Though everyone else desert you, I will not desert you!" Jesus predicts that Peter will fall away before morning. The soldiers appear and drag Jesus away for death. Peter, with the others, scurries away. Midnight finds him warming himself by a charcoal fire. There a little serving girl asks him about Jesus and devastates his resolve. Peter denies Jesus not once but thrice and melts into tears at his failure.

Sometime later Peter and the other disciples have returned to fishing. In the morning, as the sun rises, they see a figure on the beach, cooking over a charcoal fire. He graciously invites Peter to breakfast. It is none other than the Lord who presides over this meal. And then the Lord looks into this betrayer's face and commissions him to "feed my sheep." The story isn't over until God says it's over.

God is like that.

CHAPTER FOUR

CHRIST TRIUMPHANT

Believing that Christ is the salvation of the whole world, how then should we live? In an encyclical issued toward the end of his pontificate, Pope John Paul II seems to assert that the hope of universal salvation is the main impetus for the church's mission to the world:

> The Church's universal mission is born of faith in Jesus Christ, as is stated in our Trinitarian profession of faith: "I believe in one Lord, Jesus Christ, the only Son of God, eternally begotten of the Father. . . . For us men and for our salvation he came down from heaven. . . ." Each one is included in the mystery of the redemption and with each one Christ has united himself forever through this mystery. God's plan is "to gather up all things in him, things in heaven and things on earth" (Eph 1:10). . . . It is necessary to keep these two truths together, namely, the real possibility of salvation in Christ for all mankind and the necessity of the Church for salvation. . . . We know, however, that Jesus came to bring integral salvation, one which embraces the whole person and all mankind, and opens up the wondrous prospect of divine filiation. Why mission? Because to us, as to St. Paul, "this grace was given, to preach to the Gentiles the unsearchable riches of Christ" (Eph 3:8). Newness of life in him is the "Good News" for men and women of every age: all are called to it and destined for it.[1]

One reason that Christians tend to move toward those on the boundaries, tend to feel responsibility for the hungry and the dispossessed is because we worship the sort of God who has moved toward us while we were famished and out on the boundaries. God looks upon us all, even us fortunate ones, as the hungry and dispossessed who need saving. This is just the sort of God who commands, "when you give a banquet, invite the poor, the crippled, the lame, and the blind. And you will be blessed" (Luke 14:13-14). Here is a God who, for some reason known only to the Trinity, loves to work the margins inhabited by the poor, the orphaned, and the widowed; the alien and sojourner; the dead and the good as dead in the ditch. It is of the nature of this God not only to invite the poor and dispossessed but also to be poor and dispossessed, to come to the margins, thus making the marginalized the center of his realm. "Truly I tell you, just as you did it unto the least of these . . . you did it unto me" (Matt 25:40).

The story "I once was lost but now am found" is the narrative that gives us a peculiar account of lost and found, a special responsibility to seek and to save the lost. If we want to be close to Jesus—and that's a good definition of a Christian, someone who wants to go where Jesus is—then we've got to go where he goes. Christians go to church in order never to forget that we were strangers and aliens out on the margins (Eph 2:19).

"You know the heart of an alien, for you were aliens in the land of Egypt" (Exod 23:9). We were lost and then found. That continuing memory of the dynamic of our salvation—lost then found—gives us a special relationship to the lost, the poor, and anybody who does not know the story of a God who, at great cost, reaches far out in order to bring to close embrace.

In one of the most notable and depressing failures in all of the Gospels, a rich man comes to Jesus asking, "Good teacher, what must I do to inherit eternal life?" (Luke 18:18), that is, what must I do to be saved? Jesus, who appears to have a low tolerance for rich, upwardly mobile, spiritual eager beavers at first brushes him off with, "Why do you call me good? Nobody is good but God." Not the most promising of beginnings for a thoughtful dialogue on religion.

Then Jesus merely repeats the demand that he obey all the commandments of God, perhaps thinking that will end the conversation. To Jesus' surprise, the man says that he has obeyed and never once broken all the commandments since he was a kid in Sabbath school. Who among us could say that?

Jesus, undeterred by the man's apparent spiritual success and lack of need (if he's that good, what on earth could Jesus add to his goodness?) thunders, "Go, sell all that you have and give it to the poor, then come, follow me." With that radical command to redistribute his wealth, the man slumped down and got depressed, muttering to himself, "I thought Jesus was a nice person." He climbs into his Porsche and departs.

Which leads Jesus to mutter, loud enough for all his disciples to hear, "You just can't save the rich people!" He compares the salvation of the rich to shoving a fully loaded dromedary through the narrow needle's eye. It's then that the disciples ask, "Who then can be saved?"

Jesus playfully replies that with God all things "are possible," even the seeming impossible camel-through-the-eye-of-the-needle salvation of rich people. The future is possible because of the relentless desire of a loving God to get what God, in the end, wants.

God has created us as relatively free beings who can make relatively free choices and decisions, including the choice to attempt to live our lives without God. Note that I say that we are "relatively free." Christians are relativists, believing that who we are and what we can do in life is related to a Jew from Nazareth. To reject the salvation that is offered in Jesus Christ would be a tragic decision, a slap in God's face. Yet it is hard to know just what such a human decision means, in the final scheme of things. Scripture is clear that our human decisions are relative to all the decisions that God is making for us. We made a tragic decision when we not only slapped the Son of God in the face but also crucified him on a cross. And yet that cruel stupidity on our part was challenged, defeated, and blocked by the raising of crucified Jesus from the dead.

The great Jewish theologian Franz Rosenzweig, who described Christianity as a "perpetual journey of salvation," said that Islam and Christianity could never get along because Islam had no theological means of comprehending how the failings of human beings "arouse divine love more powerfully than their merits."[2]

So forgive Christians for not being overly impressed with human evil, human stupidity, and human rejection of God's abundant initiatives toward us. We live within a story of a God who, hanging upon the cross we raised against him, looked down upon his crucifiers saying, "Father, forgive them; for they do not know what they are doing" and to the thief beside him, "today you will be with me in Paradise" (Luke 23:34, 43).

Charles Wesley was inspired by the expansive vision of Ephesians 3:17-19 to write this hymn that celebrates a range and scope of divine love that is so high and so deep as to be humanly incomprehensible:

> What shall I do, my God, to love,
>   My loving God to praise?
> The length, and breadth, and height to prove,
>   And depth of sovereign grace?
> Thy sovereign grace to all extends,
>   Immense and unconfined;
> From age to age it never ends;
>   It reaches all mankind.

Throughout the world its breadth is known,
    Wide as infinity;
So wide it never passed by one,
    Or it had passed by me.
The depth of all-redeeming love
    What angel tongue can tell?
O may I to the utmost prove
    The gift unspeakable.
Deeper than hell, it plucked me thence;
    Deeper than inbred sin,
Jesus' love my heart shall cleanse
    When Jesus enters in.
Come quickly, gracious Lord, and take
    Possession of Thine own;
My longing heart vouchsafe to make
    Thine everlasting throne.[3]

Knowing what we do of the loving *eros* of God in Christ, should we pray for the salvation of all? Jesus clearly commands us to love our neighbor, which might be reason enough to pray for the salvation of all. The astounding thing is that Jesus commanded us even to pray for our enemies. Jesus' demand that we pray for our enemies is a teaching that is virtually unknown in any other faith that is alternative to Christianity. (I'm disturbed that in many churches where I pray, the prayers seem to be exclusively for the health and wholeness of those within that congregation—a far cry from the church that is commanded to pray for our enemies.) Jesus' demand to love enemies and pray for those who persecute would, I suppose, include loving God's enemies and persecutors as well.

It would have been so much easier if Jesus had merely asked us to get along with our enemies. Tolerance is an Enlightenment virtue, the best that can be mustered by those who do not know a merciful God. Divine love is considerably more demanding than simple tolerance. Those whom we love, we quite naturally desire to be saved. As Christians, we are trying to love a God who desires to love all. We want what God wants; therefore, if we pray, "Thy will be done on earth as it is in heaven," then we ought to pray that God's will be done and that all will be saved. How seldom one hears a really good prayer for Osama bin Laden, despite Jesus' command and Paul's conviction that, in the end, Jesus shall not only triumph for the elect but shall also destroy "every ruler and every authority and power" handing over all earthly powers, including Al-Qaeda, "to God the Father" (1 Cor 15:24).

David Willis emends with brackets the first question of the Heidelberg Catechism in order to stress the universal, communal implications of our conviction that God has in Christ come out and grabbed us—all:

"What is your only comfort in life and death?" "That I [and my loved ones, and my enemies, and ultimately the whole of creation] belong body and soul, in life and in death, not to myself [ourselves] but to my [our] faithful Savior Jesus Christ who at the cost of his own blood has full paid for all my [our] sins."[4]

At one time my church had missionaries in places like Iran and Iraq, courageous people who lovingly, nonviolently tried to tell and to demonstrate to all the love of God in Jesus Christ. We have no missionaries there now. We acquiesced to our government's desire to handle enemies Caesar's way rather than Jesus' way. Of course, God is not only loving but also powerful; therefore, God can work wonders despite us and our lack of concern for those who don't know of their salvation in Christ. Yet I doubt we made Jesus' saving work with the Iranians and Iraqis any easier by our belligerent destruction and mayhem, even for the best of our motives.

Do we find it so easy to do things Caesar's way because of our lousy theology of salvation? Two errors among us ought to be noted:

1. When push comes to shove, and our national well-being is threatened, we really don't believe that God "desires all to be saved and to come to the knowledge of the truth," nor do we believe that God is able to accomplish God's desires. So we treat others as irretrievably among the damned and, therefore, as potential targets for our bombs.
2. Salvation has somehow gotten either radically personalized—something that applies to me and my family in a purely individual way, without cosmic consequence—or radically nationalized—the government is my most cherished source of ultimate security and hope (that is, salvation) and must be defended with murderous intensity.

I couldn't figure out the vitriolic intensity for religions that characterizes Christopher Hitchens's wickedly funny, mean-spirited *God Is Not Great: How Religion Poisons Everything*.[5] I can't imagine that Hitchens's buddies at *Vanity Fair* are in danger of religion being too strong an influence on their lives, but perhaps I'm selling them short. Are people who believe in a god so menacing to the intellectual establishment that Hitchens must be enlisted to trash them? Then I read Hitchens's skilled defense, in *Vanity Fair,* of the trashing of Iraq, and I got it—the penny dropped. If we are going to unite this country, marching in step as one, so convinced of our righteousness and of the impossibility of any solution to the world's problems other than what we impose, then we can't have anyone running around loose who believes that ultimately there may be some judge more authoritative and truthful than public opinion this week. One of the greatest challenges of being Christian today is to believe that the sovereign God who died on the cross for the whole world is jealous of national sovereignty.

In Romans 5:12-21 the word *all* is repeated five times, as if it were a litany, as if Paul really wanted to stress that word *all* to people like us whose world is circumscribed within national boundaries. It is difficult to restrict the use of the word *all* to make it mean *some* or even *many.* When Christ tells us to "take courage," because he has "conquered the world" (John 16:33), does he really mean that we should take courage because he has conquered a great deal of the world?

ALL?

A Christian is not saved in order to be plucked out of the damned rabble of humanity, but rather is saved in order to be truly *for* humanity. The church is the community that lives ahead of time, the people who say now what may one day be said by all, once God gets what God wants—"Your kingdom come. Your will be done, on earth as it is in heaven" (Matt 6:10). Christians have been let in on an open secret, a secret that we are called to make public. If we pray for the salvation of all we pray on the basis of our hope for the reconciliation of all, for how is it possible to pray for what you don't hope?

Martin Luther and John Wesley affirmed the universality and all-inclusiveness of the electing and reconciling work of God, though in different ways; it's all grace for all, though not all are for grace. As I have noted, Calvin taught "limited atonement"; it's all grace, but grace is not for all. Although I can appreciate Calvin's determination to guard God's sovereign freedom to say yes and to say no, I confess that I don't see where Calvin finds his "double predestination" (God predetermines some for salvation, some for damnation) in Scripture. I can understand the some for salvation and some for damnation, but it's the predetermination that seems an undue limitation upon the freedom of a sovereign, resourceful, and (in my experience) relentless Savior.

Unlike Calvin, I hear only one side of "double predestination" in this passage of Paul:

> Blessed be the God and Father of our Lord Jesus Christ, who has blessed us in Christ with every spiritual blessing in the heavenly places, just as he chose us in Christ before the foundation of the world to be holy and blameless before him in love. He destined us for adoption as his children through Jesus Christ, according to the good pleasure of his will, to the praise of his glorious grace that he freely bestowed on us in the Beloved. (Eph 1:3-6)

"Destined" sounds coercive, forced. Forced into what? Forced to be "adopted as children"? Sad, when Paul appears to have intended "predestination" as praise for the determination of Christ to be for us "in love," some (Darby, the Plymouth Brethren) interpret this to mean that some are locked out. I hear divine endurance and perseverance being stressed in Ephesians 1:3-6, not exclusion. Texts come to mind such as Paul's great hymn to the persistence of God's unifying intent: "[nothing] will be able to separate us from the love of God in Christ Jesus our Lord" (Rom 8:39). Then there's Matthew's, "And remember, I am with you always, to the end of the age" (Matt 28:20).

Jesus Christ—the seeking shepherd, the waiting father, the searching woman, the persistent presence until the end of the age—is the majestic, all-powerful, sweeping generalization. He is the "Yes!" of God pronounced upon the whole broken world. Yet there is also our frail, responsive, small, but essential "yes." God's grand decision for us precedes our decisions for God. We can say "yes" only because God has said "Yes!" to us in Christ.

> As surely as God is faithful, our word to you has not been "Yes and No." For the Son of God, Jesus Christ, whom we proclaimed among you, Silvanus and Timothy and I, was not "Yes and No"; but in him it is always "Yes." For in him every one of God's promises is a "Yes." For this reason it is through him that we say the "Amen," to the glory of God. But it is God who establishes us with you in Christ and has anointed us, by putting his seal on us and giving us his Spirit in our hearts as a first installment. (2 Cor 1:18-21)

We are the first installment of a debt that has been and is being paid. The battle is not between equals, but it is still a fierce fight. Our redemption is a fact, though a not yet fully accomplished, utterly finished fact. This is a hopeful word to the world. The pain and injustice that we experience are not illusory, not fake. They are reminders that we are not there, have not arrived at the completeness of what God has in store for us, not yet. The divine verdict upon our sin has been reached—all are prisoners, all receive mercy—yet not all know that divine decree, not all live in the light of that decision. For those of us who know, those who don't know are our great burden and delight, our assignment, and our gift.

We are therefore not to take smug consolation in our knowledge of salvation. Rather, we are commissioned to "go," and to "tell" (Matthew 28:19-20). Evangelism is driven by the engine of God's salvation that demands to be announced to all. We neither rest nor retreat until every corner of God's creation gets the news of God's salvation. One reason why the church flags in its evangelistic drive is its mediocre soteriology. When God's great "Yes" degenerates into a constrained "perhaps," there is little urgency to tell the world. What we have to say to the world is deflated into a message about just another technique alongside all the others that that the world is busy pursuing already. This is not news. What's news is that in Jesus Christ God was reconciling the world to himself.

Although Ephesians 2:8 says, "this is not your own doing" but it is the "gift of God," revivalism, beginning in the nineteenth century (heritage of Charles Finney, Dwight Moody, Billy Graham, and others), put too much responsibility for salvation upon the shoulders of converts. When modern evangelicals beg people to "make a decision for Christ," I fear that they are playing into the hands of consumeristic North American capitalism. Our country has become a vast supermarket of desire in which empty people rush to and fro attempting to grab as much as we can, hoping to choose that which would make our lives worth living. As we have noted, we love thinking of ourselves as fabricators of our lives through our astute choices and decisions. I am who I decide to be. Evangelicals who exalt human choice and personal decision are unwittingly continuing the worst tendencies of discredited liberalism—all truth is decided and chosen by the sovereign self and its allegedly "free" choices.

Christian salvation is another view of humanity that arises out of faith in a God who has chosen to be for us. Our lives are not the sum of our choices, but rather the results of the impact of God's grace upon us. Evangelism is an imaginative act that enables people to describe their lives in the light of the purpose of the world. For some, that narrative will mean relinquishment, letting go of their false and erroneous loyalties in light of the good news. For others it will be the embrace of something fresh and new, a living into a whole new world. Still others will experience it as a new sense of themselves as valued, cherished people who now have a self-knowledge that the world could not give them. The existence that once was outside them (the salvation wrought by Jesus Christ in cross and resurrection) will now be internalized, igniting them, so much so that they may speak of having been thereby "born again," as if their previous existence were one great confusion, nothing to compare with their lives having been found by the searching shepherd, the seeking woman, the waiting father, the inviting boss, the reckless farmer.

Does affirmation of the ultimate triumph of God in Jesus Christ, and the possibility that all might be saved, mean that human beings are rendered irresponsible, that grace is ultimately irresistible? Our salvation is a gift, and yet it is a gift that is offered along with God's gift of human freedom. If God loves us in freedom, then the very nature of grace entails the possibility of refusal and rejection. If grace is automatic or assumed, it tends to be neither gracious nor grace. John Wesley (along with Paul) taught that even our receptivity to the gift of grace is also a sign of the working of grace.

We Wesleyans believe that salvation in Jesus Christ need not be a single, momentous, all-at-once affair. In the Eucharist we acclaim that Jesus Christ has come and has overcome, and is yet to come and will overcome. As 1 Peter 1:20 put it, "He was destined before the foundation of the world, but was revealed at the end of the ages for your sake." Furthermore, Jesus is depicted as calling each person by name, each in our own way, each in our own time. The experience of salvation can be momentous, instantaneous; but more typically it will be a matter of sequence and process. As Karl Barth put it, "[God] is not like a school master who gives the same lesson to the whole class, or an officer who moves his whole squadron in the same direction, or a bureaucrat."[6]

So Barth warns us not to build fences around God's grace by making God's grace into a general principle whereby either salvation or damnation is inevitable for everyone no matter what. Christian salvation is not an idea but an agent. Some form of universalism is always possible for those who are convinced of the persistence and are hopeful for the ultimate triumph of God's grace. Yet there is also an inevitable tension in the possibility of an incontrovertible rejection of grace by a sinful human being. Sin in this context is any human opposition to the prior divine disposition to be God *pro nobis*. *Sin* is a name for the various human forms of "no" in the face of God's "yes." If there is some sort of universal restoration and salvation, Barth said "it can only be a matter of the unexpected work of grace" working upon a disobedient and death-deserving humanity.[7]

The book of Job raises a question, in a sense, a difficult, unanswerable question of justice: why do the wicked prosper (21:7)? Job notes that God appears to subject both the wicked and the good to equal hardships (9:22). Job says that God has treated him badly, for he is a good and blameless man whom God has made a laughingstock before the wicked (12:4-6). Job flatly declares that God has attacked, humiliated, and hated him (16:7-9). If Job can't blame God for his plight, whom ought he to blame, for God is at the heart of everything (12:7-25)? In his anger and hurt at God, Job calls for a public hearing with God (13:3), a time to put God in the dock for a cross-examination (9:20-21).

God never questions Job's protestations of innocence. Guilt or innocence, goodness or badness doesn't seem to be of great interest to God in the book of Job. Finally, when God speaks to Job, it is out of a whirlwind, and God doesn't talk about guilt. God brashly asserts cosmic lordship and ridicules Job's smallness in the great scheme of things and never really entertains any of Job's searching questions. The God who meets Job in the whirlwind seems beyond and above any philosophical answer, certainly above easy moral calculations about the deserving or undeserving of reward and punishment. The God of the whirlwind is loud and swaggering, leaving nothing settled or stable while speaking.

And yet, after Job's failed attempts to dialogue, what is there? Communion and communication with God. No philosophical, reasoned response is given to Job's searching questions. Something better is given. God. There is presence, availability (38:1; 42:1-6). God speaks personally to Job, restores not only Job's fortunes but more important, a relationship. Job says that previously he had *heard* of God. Now he sees God (42:5).

I take this as a kind of parable of the way salvation is sometimes experienced. Some people are terribly and undeniably battered by life. It is only natural that they should feel enmity toward the giver and author of life. They want answers. They yearn for vindication. Rarely, from what I have observed, are they given answers. They are given God. The gods of the Greeks, when things get bad, drop down occasionally from heaven, *deus ex machina*. This God saves by being there, with us. Salvation is no mere tallying to determine guilt or innocence. Salvation is finally being with God, God coming to us in our need, and then our wonderment at the greatness of God, reveling in the mystery. The mystery that previously was a threat, a dilemma, now, in salvation, in the presence of God, is a great joy. This is what Wesley called God's "darling attribute"—"universal love."[8]

First Peter believes that this divine reach extends even to the dead where Jesus preached "to the spirits in prison, who in former times did not obey," so that, they who "had been judged . . . might live . . . as God does" (1 Pet 3:19-20; 4:6). This was known as the harrowing of hell, when Jesus went down in death, even to hell, to reach out to those who, because of chronology, knew nothing of him or his saving work.

Paul speaks about death being "swallowed up in victory" (1 Cor 15:54); "what is mortal" is "swallowed up by life" (2 Cor 5:4). It is a fascinating metaphor of divine voraciousness. Paul cannot get enough of this sort of praising of the victory of Christ that removes the sting of death, disarms and unmasks the principalities and powers, and makes a ridiculous spectacle of them.

Jesus' love for sinners goes beyond all of our boundaries, including those of our limited imagination. Jesus demonstrates not only a God who loves sinners, but a God who ridiculously, extravagantly, recklessly, actively loves. So why should the reckless reach of such love not be as far even as hell? This led the church to say that Christ conquers not only the world but also hell. He was not content to rest with partial triumph. That which for us was a dark, fearful abyss has become for him a path to us, the way he makes to complete triumph.

I remember a play that I saw when I was in college, a play that I've never been able to relocate—perhaps I dreamed it? At any rate, it was a drama of a poor, tormented man who went on, and on in the drama about his misery and bad state of mind. He wants to end his life, but he has nagging fears that if he commits suicide, he may go to hell. Finally he cannot take any more of life and, putting a pistol to his head, he fires. There is a loud explosion and the stage becomes completely dark. Then after a few moments, the lights come on again, and we see the man lying face down on the stage, pistol in his hand. Behind him is a bald-headed man seated behind an office desk. The man behind the desk says to the man lying on the stage, "Well, Mr. Jones. Are your theatrics ended? Gabriel, bring me the file on Jones. Mr. Jones, please take a seat here. We've got all the time in the world to talk things out."

Jones stirs, looks out at the audience in complete horror as the curtain comes down. Is this "hell"—to be condemned to an eternity to be exposed totally to the God who has stalked us throughout life? At last to be forced to be in conversation with the one we have been so long avoiding? It's a disturbing, invigorating thought.

THE CHURCH AND SALVATION

Jesus says, in John's Gospel, "when I am lifted up . . . [I] will draw all people to myself" (John 12:32). Like a great magnet that picks up all kinds of metallic trash indiscriminately, Jesus says that when he is lifted up (and how he was lifted up!) he will indiscriminately draw all to himself. All. The great thing about being in the church is to get a front row seat on his magnetic drawing all unto himself. As a pastor I've seen them slip through the cracks, ripped violently through the eye of the needle or caught in the great dragnet, cut down, and gathered for the harvest, pursued all the way into the wilderness, drawn unto him. It is for me living proof that God was in Christ reconciling the world.

"Lift up your hearts" is the way the pastor invites the congregation to prayer.

"We lift them up to the Lord," the people respond. Any thought about salvation in the name of Jesus is an exercise in *Sursum corda*. "Stand up and raise your heads, because your redemption is drawing near" (Luke 21:28). "I lift up my eyes" (Ps 121:1). When we look up to God, we are looking for salvation, looking in expectation that our salvation comes from outside ourselves.

> The eyes of all look to you,
> and you give them their food in due season.
> You open your hand,
> satisfying the desire of every living thing. (Ps 145:15-16)

Christ gives so much of himself to us that those of us who share the Eucharist speak of feeding on him (John 6). The self-giving of this God, God's determination to be intimate with us, is virtually without limit, so much so that Jesus said, "I'm the bread of life. Feed on me!"

Pseudo-Dionysius (in *De Divinis nominibus*, "The Divine Names") rhapsodizes upon the alluring love of God that seeks deep union with every living thing:

> The Good returns all things to itself and gathers together whatever may be scattered. . . . Each being looks to it as a source, as the agent of cohesion, and as an objective. The Good, as scripture testifies, produced

everything and . . . in it, "all things hold together" [Col 1:17] and are maintained and preserved as if in some almighty receptacle. All things are returned to it as their own goal. All things desire it: Everything sentient years to perceive it, everything lacking perception has a living and instinctive longing for it, and everything lifeless and merely existent turns, in its own fashion, for a share of it.[9]

Like a great magnet, drawing all through the narrow needle's eye, ensnaring, reaching, embracing, constantly moving down toward those in the ditch in order to pull up all, gathering up all in the dance. All.

Isaiah hears Yahweh declare, "For a brief moment I abandoned you, but with great compassion I will gather you" (54:7). This gathering of God is church. On the cross, after Jesus had said and done all, he receives a positive response but from one poor, penitent thief who hangs in agony beside him. It was to this thief that he promised, "Today you will be with me in Paradise" (Luke 23:43). Barth said that this is the formation of the first church, the result of God's cosmic salvage operation. God salvages the refuse of the world, reconstitutes and gathers the lost. To the exiles Isaiah proclaims:

> See, the Lord GOD comes with might,
>   and his arm rules for him; . . .
> He will feed his flock like a shepherd;
>   he will gather the lambs in his arms,
> and carry them in his bosom,
>   and gently lead the mother sheep. (Isa 40:10-11)

And so I stand on Sunday before the table of the Lord and look out upon the gathered congregation. My pastoral perch is a good vantage point from which to assess the scope of God's saving work. From what I can see on Sunday, Jesus has gathered about him an insufficiently culled harvest. A motley crew, they are young and old, dignified and ridiculous, knowledgeable of Scripture and ignorant, well-informed and clueless. See them drawn toward the throne. They are all being drawn in the great dragnet of God's grace, all being pulled through the narrow needle's eye, all drawn by the majestic, bloody magnet of love that is Jesus Christ. All.

We have tried carefully to teach them to receive the sacrament standing up, hands outstretched. We have told them that contemporary liturgical reform has overcome our former penitential obsession at the Lord's Supper. But they are Methodists. They love to kneel for the Body and the

Blood. They throw themselves down at the altar, doing with their bodies what they have only felt in their hearts and more than they have reasoned in their brains. The church has failed them in so many ways but at least the church has taught them this: they are empty-handed beggars, starving for food that they cannot obtain on their own. They must stoop a bit to receive this blessing from the one who blessed the spiritually poor. In a consumptive economy, just to know that is great wisdom.

Watch them kneel and hold out their hands in grateful wonder. They thrust forth their hands toward the table in eagerness. They come reaching for the gifts of bread and wine, as if their embrace by the suffering beggar who was the Son of God were the most natural thing in the world, as if Jesus died for them alone. There are so many differently reaching hands, so multifarious an array of need brought to the altar. I know them well enough to know that they come with wildly divergent understandings and misunderstandings of Jesus. And still Jesus feeds them all, giving them a small foretaste on this Sunday of that banquet that he intends to lavish upon them for all eternity. All.

Thus we can admit that something like "universal salvation" is a fair implication of what we know of Jesus as well as what he taught. To deny universal salvation as implication and possibility, as hope and desire, is to limit and to restrict the power and grace of God. To assert with absolute certainty universal salvation is to restrict the freedom and grace of God. Still, we may, indeed we ought, to hope and to pray and to work for what we hope.

How does the story of the prodigal son end? It doesn't really have a conclusive ending. The parable ends, not with the prodigal and his friends partying together, but rather with the father out in the darkness, pleading with the older brother to come in and join the party. The father does not simply rejoice that his younger son is home. Nor does the father condemn the older brother to hell because he refuses to come celebrate the return of the prodigal. It isn't that the father loves one son and not the other. The father loves both sons and is determined to give them what they need to join the party. To the younger he gives his whole inheritance and a party; to the older he gives reassurance, "Son, you are always with me" (Luke 15:31). He gives more than an invitation; he actively pleads with his older son to come to the party.

Did the older son ever relent and join the merriment? Perhaps Jesus did not end the story because God's loving work with us doesn't end. Only God can give an ending. The father is not only the one who decrees forgiveness of past sin but is also the one who ventures into the darkness and actively pleads with us to come to the party. And that's why we cannot pronounce some last word on the possibility of the salvation of all. The story continues, in your life and mine, maybe even in your death and mine, because the story of the possibility of our eternal destiny isn't over until God says it's over, until God gets as much a victory as God wants.

In this book I've made a great deal of Jesus' parables as gracious narrative representations of the mystery of our salvation. Sometimes Christians get to become gracious parables of salvation in Christ:

"Our son has been putting us through hell," she said. "Didn't even know where he was for months until last night. My husband and I were eating dinner, and suddenly, without warning, he bursts through the front door and begins cursing us, demanding money, refusing to join us at the table. After an ugly scene, he stormed down the hall and slammed the door to his room."

It's sad what parents are sometimes forced to endure from their children.

"Well, my husband gets up, goes over to the kitchen, pours himself a drink, turns on the TV, and slumps down in his chair. That's how he handles these moments. I walked down the hall and said, 'Son, can we talk? I just want to talk.' I could hear him curse me from inside his bedroom. I tried to open the door. It was locked.

"So I went into the garage, got a big hammer, walked back in, stood before my son's bedroom door, drew back, and with only one blow was able to knock the doorknob clean off the door. Took about a third of the door with it. Then I lunged at my surprised-looking son, grabbed him around the throat, and said, 'I'm not going to put up with this shit anymore. You are better than this! I gave birth to you, went into labor for you, and I'm not giving you away!'

"I really think something important happened for us last night. I think he heard me. We're on a new track," she said.

I believe God is something like that.

CHAPTER FIVE

DAMNED?

I know what you are thinking. While lauding the triumph of Christ in the reconciliation of the world, aren't there many assertions in the New Testament that some, perhaps many, might be damned—the sheep separated from the goats, the wheat from the tares; many on the broad road to hell and few ascending the narrow path to salvation? These texts suggest a well-populated hell. It's enough to make us ask, "will only a few be saved?" (Luke 13:23). Jesus responded to the query with talk of a "narrow door" in which many "will not be able" to enter (Luke 13:24). How narrow is that door?

Hell is the opposite of heaven. Hell is that eternal separation that is contrary to what God wants: eternal reconciliation. If we have little firsthand experience of heaven, that time and place where God is all in all, we know next to nothing, since Jesus came among us, of hell, that time and place where God is not. It is the nature of the risen Christ to intrude, to encroach upon empty places of the heart, to fill each drab void with radiant light. So forgive Christians for not knowing much about hell—the void where love is not, where Christ's victory is null. Those of us who have been stalked by the risen Christ tend to believe that it is difficult for any human to keep the Hound of Heaven forever at bay.

And yet the God who loves us has made us as those who are able to turn aside from God's move toward us, those who are able to refuse God's outstretched hand. I am reluctant to call such stupid refusal an aspect of God-given freedom, for it hardly seems "free" to reject whom God created you to be. How odd that the creature who is created to be with the Creator is (in the words of the old hymn) "prone to wander." Something in us finds it quite attractive at last to be where God is silenced, and we are free at last to be as we damn well please. C. S. Lewis said that, in hell, the door is locked from the inside.[1]

Was the psalmist celebrating or perhaps complaining when he sang these verses:

> Where can I go from your spirit?
>   Or where can I flee from your presence?
> If I ascend to heaven, you are there;
>   if I make my bed in Sheol, you are there. (Ps 139:7-8)

Something in us does not want the God who wants us. The rich man, when offered eternal life, walked in the other direction, finding his stuff more loveable than Jesus. Thus hell remains a real, but nevertheless inexplicable, possibility, a failure not of the resourceful love of God, but rather of our own disordered desire. Hell is getting what you think you really want. In Dante's *Inferno* those whose main pleasure was lust are allowed to burn forever and gluttons are doomed to unending engorgement. The heaven we craved is the hell we got.

There are those who charge some contemporary renditions of the Christian faith as being insipid and inconsequential because today's Christians are squeamish about divine punishment for sin. One can see their point. Just before we attempt to pass judgment upon him, Jesus speaks of the separation of the sheep from the goats on the last day (Matt 25:31-46) where the goats are condemned "into eternal punishment, but the righteous into eternal life" (25:46). (I noted that when guest preachers to the pulpit of our university chapel picked their scripture, this text was their favorite. I've heard Matthew 25:31-46 used to condemn Ronald Reagan's welfare policies, Margaret Thatcher's administration, and even Bill Clinton's first budget to Congress. Contemporary self-described "progressive Christians" may not be opposed to hell if they can determine hell's inhabitants!)

Recently, a professor of Islamic studies at the University of North Carolina, in a radio interview, declared, "If you live a good and righteous life here on earth then hopefully there will be no surprises in the afterlife."[2] He was obviously not talking about the Christian faith where, according to Matthew 25, there will be surprises for everyone! Surprising Jesus was notorious for welcoming whores into the kingdom of God and telling the presumed righteous that they could go to Gehenna. The Judge who sits on the throne surprises because his judgments are unlike ours.

Please note that in Jesus' parable, both the blessed sheep and the cursed goats are *ignorant*—both ask, "Lord, when did we see you?" Neither the sheep nor the goats were out looking for Jesus, nor did they know Jesus when he stood before them. Both were encountered by him incognito as he pushed into their lives in the faces of the poor, the imprisoned, and famished. This suggests to me that the parable of the Great Judgment is not a lesson in how to shape up and, therefore, avoid God's judgment but rather a statement on the impossibility of circumventing God's judgment. We *shall be judged*, says the parable, no matter how zealously you worked for the defeat of George Bush or the hours you gave to Habitat for Humanity. And the judgments shall be those of God, not those urged by either progressive or conservative preachers. (I note in passing that, alas, in Matthew's story, no one appears to be numbered among the saved on the basis of having read a book on salvation!)

In a lifetime of attempts to preach, I've preached fewer than a dozen sermons on hell and damnation, which seems just about right to me. We should not hesitate to talk about God's punishment, as long as we speak about it as the Bible speaks and with no more frequency or enthusiasm than Jesus. The churches' beliefs about hell may owe more to Augustine's *Enchiridion* than to Scripture.[3] Augustine's insights on hell made their way into the so-called Athanasian Creed (ca. 381–428) where it was affirmed, "At his coming all human beings shall rise with their bodies and . . . those who have done evil will go into everlasting fire." Luther and Calvin had no problem in affirming eternal punishment by Satan of those who "have done evil." How could God be just if God allows evil people to get away with evil, forever?

Though it is possible to find about two hundred references to the fate of those who are "lost" in the New Testament, Augustine bases his hell argument mainly on Matthew 25:31-46. For reasons noted above, this is a questionable Augustinian move; Matthew 25 is a parable, not a well-worked-out doctrine of faith or a legal formula.

The idea of eternal punishment was challenged by Origen (ca. 185–254) who argued for some sort of *apokatastasis*, the final restoration of all things. Though Origen's ideas (or at least what the church understood of them) were condemned at Constantinople in 543, and though he had some strange metaphysics backing up his soteriology, I think we ought to listen to Origen one more time. Origen agreed that God's love must take sin and rebellion seriously but stressed that God in Christ has a peculiar way of taking our sin and rebellion seriously. Origen agreed that hell is real but disagreed that it was eternal. Hell is more a purifying fire than eternal torment, more educative than retributive. The fire is God who purifies sinners. Hell is more remedial than retributive, a kind of horribly bitter pill that is taken in order to cure us of our sin and its effects. Paul says that Christian leaders who are unfaithful (bishops take note!) must be purged and thereby "will be saved, but only as through fire" (1 Cor 3:15).

When someone is "lost" does that mean simply that he or she has not yet been found? Origen expects that the torment of bishops and other sinners will not last forever. In a crescendo of divine resolve, all shall be restored. God's punishment is not an end in itself but is yet another example of the ways that God weaves even the worst of calamities into God's good purposes. Until that time of eventual restoration, the drift of sinners into hell and the torments endured there must bring torment to the loving Savior, if the Savior's goal is to save, to return all things and all people to the perfect harmony that the Creator intended at the beginning. Origen taught this, not on the basis of any sentimental or optimistic assessment of human nature but rather on the basis of his unqualified faith in the essential benevolence and mercy of God.

Jesus instructed his followers on how we are to handle injustices done toward one another in the church (Matt 18:15-22). The offender is to be judgmentally confronted. If he refuses to repent, even when implored by the whole church, then Jesus says to treat him as if he were a "Gentile and a tax collector." This sounds at first like Jesus saying, "If he refuses to shape up, to hell with him," justice must be served. But then we remember that Jesus was crucified, in great part, because of his persistent carousing with Gentiles and tax collectors. We must deal with Gentiles and tax collectors as Jesus dealt with them—by going to parties with them.

One place where hell is mentioned by Jesus (or at least "Hades") is Luke 16:19-31 where a rich man dies and goes to Hades and a poor man dies and is "carried away by the angels to be with Abraham" (v. 22). Just as a great gap of economic inequality separated these two men in life so a great gap of divine retribution separates them in the afterlife. When the rich man cries out in his torment to Father Abraham, the blessed patriarch says casually that, whereas the poor man Lazarus was in torment in his earthly life, the rich man had a sort of heaven on earth with enough to eat and fine clothes to wear. Now the tables have been turned in God's justice. End of discussion.

As a rich person with enough food and clothes, will I be told that God has already given me my heavenly reward? This is as good as it gets? It's a hell of a thought.

Slaves, working out in the cotton fields on a hot Sunday morning in the Old South, looked up from their forced labor. They saw the master and his family getting into their fine coach, wearing their nice clothes, and preparing to go to their fine church for Sunday morning worship. One of the slaves began singing the spiritual, "Everybody Talkin' 'bout Heaven Ain't a-Goin' There."

At other times they sang, "I got shoes, you got shoes, all God's children got shoes. And when I get to heaven, gonna put on my shoes, I'm gonna walk all over God's heaven." That was the song of slaves, many of whom did not have shoes in this world. Hell is that time and place where those who have had everything that this world can give are made to see the poverty of their lives. Heaven is that time and that place where those who had to go barefoot in this world, at last have shoes. Heaven is the delightful, disarming place and time where God gets what God wants.

As he was led away to be hanged by the Nazis, Alfred Depp—friend of Bonhoeffer and powerful preacher—said to the soldier who took him to the gallows, "In a few minutes, I'll know more than you do."

Today, in my part of the Body of Christ, sentimentality and optimistic views of human nature (all evidence from contemporary human behavior to the contrary) tend to dominate our discussions of hell. It's impossible to believe, say these theological sentimentalists, that a God as nice as ours could consign people as nice as us to eternal perdition. Human freedom and its misuse is the only possible explanation for punishment in any guise because, in the modern world, freedom is the defining human attribute. In the face of the multifarious forms of human bondage (addiction, sociological and economic determinism, genetics, and so on) and the undeniable evidence of human culpability (any evening on the nightly news) many still contend that our damnation is incredible.[4]

This is sentimentalism—the attempt not to think about the ambiguity, tragedy, and conflict that go unresolved with the realization that Jesus is God and we are not. Sentimentality arises from hunger to have God on our terms, to reduce the will of God to "what seems right to me." It is also my attempt to be near God without risk of my transformation. Even though it is disconcerting to think that I may one day be held responsible for living like the rich man who ignored the injustice committed against Lazarus, or that I failed to treat my enemies as Jesus commanded, perhaps that's what love demands.

The sweet-spirited person who crooned, "The God whom I love would never harshly judge someone, condemning him forever to punishment," is the person who, under the cover of self-ascribed compassion is awfully arrogant in demanding just what God should or shouldn't do in order to be loved. The God whom I'm trying to love is capable of doing a host of things—including judging, condemning, refining, and punishing me—things that I wouldn't do to me if I were God. Our ways are not God's ways, our thoughts not as high as God's (Isa 55:8).

The horror of life without God has lost its place in our imagination. We are little plagued by the prospect that there might be that time and that place whereby we are left to the mercy of our own devices. That's exactly where most of us strive to be—by ourselves. Garbo spoke for us all— we just want to be left alone. The hell of life without God has been transformed into the true and only heaven of modernity—blessed solitude. American theology, mocked by H. Richard Niebuhr, is us all over: "A God without wrath brought men without sin into a kingdom without judgment through the ministrations of a Christ without a cross."[5]

Despite our judgmental willingness, even eagerness to have two million Americans incarcerated, we are squeamish about God's judgment. One of the projects of the Enlightenment and its aftermath was to create a world in which we were immune from any external judgment other than that "which seems personally right to me." Kant, the intellectual father of the modern world, sought a humanity in which individuals freely applied judgments to themselves that were based upon reasonable criteria derived exclusively from themselves.

Still, all sentimentality aside, it seems to me that valid objections can be raised against Augustinian claims of eternal, widespread damnation and a crowded hell. One objection is that "eternal" is not something that is a possession of humans, be they damned or blessed. "Eternal" is a gift of a living God who raises the dead. To ascribe immortal, everlasting life to the damned seems odd. Second, advocates of this eternal, penal, irrevocable misery must surely contend with the Savior as depicted in Scripture. Jesus the Judge must be held in tension with Jesus the Savior, the Evangel, the one who was criticized, not for having too strict a standard of justice, but rather for seeking, inviting, and saving the lost.

Jesus is the Judge who is also our Advocate:

> My little children, I am writing these things to you so that you may not sin. But if anyone does sin, we have an advocate with the Father, Jesus Christ the righteous; he is the atoning sacrifice for our sins, and not for ours only but also for the sins of the whole world. (1 John 2:1-2)

I fear that Augustine allows his sense of human original sin to overcome his sense of Christ-initiated divine grace "for the sins of the whole world." Augustine gives too much credence to sinful Adam and too little to the triumphant Christ. How does Augustine know for sure that some are irretrievably damned? Damnation is possible, but is it probable? Neuhaus asks if biblical talk about hell is predictive (this is the way it shall be) or cautionary (this is the way it can be if one turns away from Christ's outstretched hand). Whereas Origen has nobody in hell, Augustine appears to have just about everybody there. How do either of them know this much?[6]

However, valid objections can be raised against the claims of contemporary sentimentalists. Jesus as the all-affirming, indulgent, and inclusive therapist must answer to Scripture's Jesus the Prophet, the Judge, the one who hated our sin enough to take its full force upon himself and save us through suffering for us and because of us. Jesus was crucified for telling judgmental stories like the one about Lazarus and the rich man. If finally our eternal destiny is in God's hands that applies both to the possibility of divine restoration and to the prospect of divine punishment. We just don't know. All we know for sure about any forecasted final judgment (on the basis of Matthew 25) is that there are large surprises because of the surprising Savior.

One of the appealing aspects of reading Origen on our eternal fate is that he manages to make his assertions with admirable intellectual modesty, refusing to explain away or to ignore that scripture that may be counter to his theological claims. He asserts, not a knock-down argument but rather a genuine, though not legally defined, hope that is based upon the identity of Jesus Christ.

My mentor in these matters is, once again, Karl Barth, who knew a great deal about Christian theology but, in discussions of our eternal damnation or reward, demonstrated uncharacteristic intellectual reticence.[7] Barth refused to lock God into either an "All are saved" or "Not all are saved" position, though I have admitted that Barth hoped for universal restoration. Barth found it difficult to believe that Christ's work for the salvation of the world will be finally thwarted. Still, the resilience and persistence of human sin is impressive. After all, we managed to hear and to see God With Us and still cried, "Crucify him!"

Barth hoped for the possibility that hell was sparsely populated, not because of his optimistic belief in human freedom and its effects, but rather because of his firm conviction in the triumph of divine grace. After all, God raised crucified Jesus from the dead. Barth rejected Origen's *apokatastasis* because he found the ancient theologian indulging in generalities and propositions that were disconnected from Scripture's specific narrative of the divine nature and work. God is a deliverer but not because God owes us deliverance. Sinners, according to Scripture, can never escape the threat of divine judgment and divine condemnation.

Note that we affirm in the Apostles' Creed that "he shall come to judge." In the end, as at the beginning, we do not come to Jesus; he comes to us. Christ the Judge is not like our judges—sitting back and dispassionately pronouncing judgment. God the seeking shepherd, the searching woman, comes to us, this time as the Judge who draws near to set things right between us and God, loving us enough to judge us. In all of Scripture, God's anticipated judgment is celebrated as a joyful event, a time when God at last actively overcomes the injustice and inequity of the world and gives evil what it deserves.

Thus Barth believed that salvation is not the removal of the threat of judgment but the accentuation and fulfillment of divine judgment. Salvation is to be face-to-face with the loving God whom we have so grievously wronged, which begins to sound somewhat like hell. I'm thinking here of Jesus' parable of the talents in which the master returns and simply asks, "What have you done with what you have been given?" (Matt 25:14-30). The thought of that question being put to me by Jesus sends shivers down my spine.

We affirm in the Creed, "He shall come to judge the quick [the living] and the dead." All. The judge is Christ, and none of us is above his assize. And none of us has advanced knowledge of the outcome. As Paul told a contentious congregation that tried to judge his worthiness as an apostle, "It is the Lord who judges me" (1 Cor 4:4).

Even though we know we shall be judged and even though we do not know with certainty the outcome of that judgment, we can have confidence and hope, because we know the Judge. If we "abide in him" we will have confidence at the day of his coming (1 John 2:28). In him "we have boldness before God" (1 John 3:21). The judge is the Christ who has gone to such extraordinary lengths to seek us and to bear the sins of all.

Confidence is not necessarily untroubled certainty. After all, the more closely we grow toward Christ, and the more we know of Christ (and by implication the more we know of ourselves) usually the more convinced we become of how far we are from Christ, how little we know of Christ, and how poorly we fulfill his will. Sometimes to be close to Jesus increases our uneasiness with Jesus. We know not only the one who is able to say "depart from me into the eternal fire . . . into eternal punishment" (Matt 25:41-46) and, "I never knew you" (Matt 7:23). We also know the one who gave himself as a ransom for all (1 Tim 2:1-6), the one who promised that he would "draw all people to [him]self" (John 12:32). We know that in Adam all have sinned, but now we know that the grace of Christ takes precedence over the sin of Adam (Rom 5:12-21). Or, as Barth preached so eloquently, "God has imprisoned all in disobedience, so that he may be merciful to all" (Rom 11:32). All.

One of the ways that Christian Scripture differs from that of Islam is that we are not permitted to know as much as Islam knows about heaven or hell. Christ's judgment is not *his* judgment if we presume to know the outcome beforehand. We must resist premature conclusion or synthesis. We are not permitted to despair, nor are we permitted to be presumptuous; that which we presume is not a gift, and despair doubts that Christ is able to accomplish his purposes. Humility is required.

It is unfortunate that theologians of the past attempted to draw too close analogies between human judgments and God's judgment. If you explain Jesus' death as a matter of satisfying, or substituting for, our sin in some forensic mechanism of divine judgment, you must also factor in the image of Jesus as waiting parent, as seeking shepherd, as dying friend. In thinking about salvation, historically the Western church has thought too much about salvation as a matter of atonement for sin, satisfaction for sin, and redemption from sin rather than a matter of solidarity with and a summons to sinners.

Jesus tells a story about slaves who are all given huge amounts of money in a grand wealth redistribution scheme. The master then leaves town. But when the master returns, there is accounting, judgment, and hell to pay for the cautious one-talent slave (Matt 25), though the master's judgment has got to be set alongside his generosity. In another parable, at the end of the day, when there is a final reckoning, the master of the vineyard calls in all the workers and pays everyone exactly the same wage, even those who have worked for only an hour (Matt 20:1-11). This is curious judgment for those who have done so little work. Then an unscrupulous manager defrauds his boss, allowing the boss's debtors to write off huge debts. At the accounting the boss *commends* him for his wisdom that is greater than the "children of light" (Luke 16:8). What sort of judge would tell such stories?

The late James Kennedy, longtime pastor of Coral Ridge Presbyterian Church, devised an effective evangelistic program called Evangelism Explosion. The lead question in reaching the unsaved through Evangelism Explosion was, "If God were to ask you, 'Why should I let you into my heaven?' what would you say?"

Presumably, Pastor Kennedy, who died while I was writing this book, fully in the presence of the Savior who told the story about the talented slaves, the overly generous master, the commendation of the unscrupulous manager, now knows why his question is irrelevant to Christian salvation.

Be certain, there will be judgment; the shape and the purpose of that divine reckoning are less sure. If my sermon on salvation is meant to relieve us of the tension of submitting to divine judgment—to settle this matter, to reduce the surprise—then this book is blasphemous. Indeed, one of the great challenges of being a Christian is to leave matters of judgment in the hands of God. "Vengeance is mine," says the Lord, "I will repay" (Rom 12:19).

John's Gospel has a dramatic judgment scene just before Jesus is condemned to death on the cross. Jesus is brought before the power of the empire to face his judgment by Pontius Pilate. John 19:13 says that, "When Pilate heard these words, he brought Jesus outside and sat on the judge's bench." In the Greek, I find unclear just who sat on "the judgment seat" (cf. 2 Cor 5:10). Pilate or Jesus? It's hard to tell who was sitting in judgment upon whom. The scene begins with Pilate judging this forlorn Galilean. But by the end of the conversation, Jesus—in both his words and in his silence—appears to have turned the tables on Pilate. Pilate begins the interrogation of Jesus from a position of power and scorn. The scene ends with Pilate impotent, vacillating, and trapped. Earlier Jesus had promised, "I came into this world for judgment so that those who do not see may see, and those who do see may become blind" (John 9:39). Jesus had a way, particularly in John's Gospel, of exposing those who thought they knew everything as those who know nothing (for instance, his almost comical conversation with Nicodemus in John 3 in which he renders a "great ruler of Israel" befuddled and confused). Just by being who he was Jesus sat in judgment upon those who thought that they were sitting in judgment on him. The same cross that is sign of the salvation of all is also sign of the downfall of the mighty (1 Cor 1:27).

Karl Barth said that we are judged by Christ's resurrection as much as by his cross. The Resurrection is God's final "verdict" upon our sin. God "judges [the world] with the aim of saving it."[8] On Easter evening the risen Christ returns to his disciples where they huddle behind locked doors (John 20), filled with fear. Indeed, they have much to fear, for they denied and deserted Jesus when the soldiers came to arrest him. Yet the risen Christ, rather than condemn their infidelity, breathes upon them, giving them the Holy Spirit, commissioning them to go into the world with the power of the keys, binding and loosening others as he has bound and loosed them in his resurrection. His return to them and his calling of them are not only his blessing of them but surely his judgment as well. As Barth said, the mercy of God *is* the wrath of God. Every *yes* of God to us is also *no* of God upon us.

"I came not to judge the world, but to save the world. The one who rejects me and does not receive my word has a judge; on the last day the word that I have spoken will serve as judge" (John 12:47-48). Judgment occurs whenever Christ clashes with our world, be that collision provoked by his cross or his resurrection. Judgment is when we can no longer avoid the realization that in Christ, God's ways are not our ways, when we know that the God whom we refused to love has refused not to be loved by us.

The same one of whom it was said "He was in the world, and the world came into being through him; yet the world did not know him" (John 1:10) is the one who declares to the rejecting world, "because I live, you also will live" (John 14:19). "In the world you face persecution. But take courage; I have conquered the world!" (John 16:33).

The God who meets us in the bloody, awful cross and in the stunning, unexpected, even undesired triumphant Resurrection is not a God for the intellectually moderate or the sentimental of heart. This God is quite capable of pronouncing an uncompromising "No!" to human aspirations to be God, even as God risks a triumphant "Yes!" to us in our misery. "For in him every one of God's promises . . . 'Yes'" (2 Cor 1:20).

"For all of us must appear before the judgment seat of Christ" (2 Cor 5:10)—good news or bad, judgment or mercy? Christians learn not to be able to tell the difference. The wrath of God is revealed from heaven (Rom 1:18). Wrath and mercy are the same heavenly action of the living God who stands resolutely above us, against us in order to be truly, completely *pro nobis*. God is determined to release us from the contradiction that enslaves us, yet the truth about us will be told and demonstrated to us. And that may be painful.

True, we who so often think that we just want to be left alone discover that sometimes it is as if God, in love, does just that. Like the waiting father in the parable of the loving son, God allows us to wander in some "far country," to wallow in the consequences of our "loose living" that we might eventually come to ourselves and return home to be welcomed with a party (Luke 15). God graciously gives us time in order that the One who is the truth may at last make a way to give us life.

Moving nearer the cross, Jesus overlooks Jerusalem and laments, "How often have I desired to gather your children together as a hen gathers her brood under her wings, and you were not willing!" (Luke 13:34). Divine love is persistent but does not bully. It seeks, invites, and gathers, but does not force. But then divine love, in love, lets us go and looks on and weeps at the consequences of our refusal: "See, your house is left to you" (Luke 13:35).

SALVATION TAKES TIME

Jesus told the one about the unproductive fig tree (Luke 13:6-9). Three years, no figs. The master orders the servant, "Cut it down" (v. 7). Time's up. But the servant pleads with the master's justifiable judgment, saying, "[allow me] to dig around it and put manure on it [and see what happens]" (v. 8). The master mercifully relents and the unproductive tree is given more time to bear fruit. Are we hearing a conversation in the heart of the Trinity between the justifiable judgments of God the Father with the pleading mercy of God the Son? God judges but does so in the mercy of God's own good time. (There's no way any self-respecting farmer would leave alone an unproductive tree for three years. The farmer in Jesus' parable is remarkable for his disinterest in productivity.)

In another parable, when the servants propose uprooting the weeds from the wheat, the master again postpones justifiable judgment, saying that he will sort it all out, but in his own good time (Matt 13:25). Judgment is promised, but not now. How long will the forbearing master wait? And what might we, just recipients of judgment, do in the meantime?

Reformed theologian Emil Brunner speaks of God's wrath toward us as God's "resistance."[9] Against the pressure of our sin, God takes time to apply a counter pressure. God's resistance to our evil tends to be considered by us, in our evil, as wrathful injustice; but, considered as a mechanism of our redemption, it is love. When you no longer believe in a God who loves to consort with and to forgive sinners, sentimentalism is about the best you can do to endure a truthful God.

Much of contemporary Christian theology in North America, when it attempts to be gracious, sentimentally portrays us as hapless victims. "My inept mama made me do it." Thus we would-be victims are offered therapy rather than salvation. Orthodox Christian theology depicts us, despite any injustices we may have suffered along life's way, as perpetrators who, deserving God's wrath, receive God's mercy. And sometimes, as we have noted, God's mercy has a way of feeling like God's wrath. God is not only Creator but also destroyer, resister, in order to be our Savior. This is the ironic word we have to proclaim when we preach Jesus Christ crucified:

For the message about the cross is foolishness to those who are perishing, but to us who are being saved it is the power of God. For it is written, "I will destroy the wisdom of the wise, and the discernment of the discerning I will thwart." Where is the one who is wise? Where is the scribe? Where is the debater of this age? Has not God made foolish the wisdom of the world? For since, in the wisdom of God, the world did not know God through wisdom, God decided, through the foolishness of our proclamation, to save those who believe. (1 Cor 1:18-21)

Salvation is painful, a blessing yes, but a gift not without cost for the giver and the gifted.

Troubled by the denial and blaming that I found in my own church in a time of decline and diminishing returns on evangelistic efforts, I consulted an organizational consultant who told me, "Every troubled organization is full of fear. In such a situation, leaders have the responsibility to face the fear and to tell the truth, to say, 'You are in denial because you are fearful that you don't have the resources to face the truth about your condition and do something about it.' A leader must put an organization in pain that it's been avoiding at all costs. The leader tells the truth out of faith that the organization already has the needed resources to face facts."

Is Christ's judgment of us a sign of Christ's faith in us? The parable of the talents—in which the master lavishes such great sums upon the servants—is not only a story of God's judgment but also of God's incredible faith in the servants. The one who judges Israel is first the one who has elected Israel. From this perspective our "damnation" is not so much a work of God but rather our arrogant refusal, our steadfast determination not to be engaged by the work of God in our salvation.

Jesus intrudes his hometown synagogue in Nazareth (Luke 4:16-30), joyously announcing the "acceptable year of the Lord" when God will at last save God's people. There is an excited stirring in the congregation. God is coming to us, God's elect, now to make good on God's promises, now to evict the Roman overlords and to give us the salvation we deserve!

Then Jesus, working exclusively from the Scriptures, begins to preach. First, he recalls God's salvations in the past. He reminds the congregation that the last time God appeared in the form of the prophet Elijah, there were many poor widows in Israel. God's prophet fed none of them. Only this widow who was an outsider. And surely there were many sick people in Israel in the days of Elisha. The prophet healed only a Syrian army officer. And the congregation's joy at the announcement of their salvation turned to wrath when they were reminded (from their own Scriptures!) that God's notion of "salvation" sometimes felt like our notion of judgment.

To be made to stand before the mirror of truth, even though it may take an eternity to face the facts about ourselves, is an aspect of God's faith in us. Though we don't believe that we have the resources to live truthfully, God believes in us more than we believe in ourselves. God is willing to take time with us. And if anyone is ever able to stand before that judging, redeeming mirror and face the facts, it is only in response to something that God enacts, not as the product of our own will or intellect. If we are able to love, it is because we have first been loved (1 John 4:19). We did not choose God, God in Christ chose us (John 15:16). Grace alone separates the lost from the found, the redeemed from those yet awaiting the full communion that God desires for all.

Love is not love that is irresponsible. Unresponsiveness is the death of a relationship. Love is not love that is unwilling to take time with the beloved. A lover who expects nothing of the beloved, who does not want the best for the beloved is not really in love. Once again the story that Jesus told of extravagant beneficence (Matt 25:14-30), his so-called parable of the talents: A man summoned his slaves and gave them everything he had, lavishing huge sums of money upon them in varying degrees. The master leaves them holding everything he owns, every cent, with no instruction on how they are to invest so much treasure. "After a long time" he returns and "settled accounts with them" (v. 19). There is graciousness and lavish gift, but there is also definitive accounting.

The master is delighted with the results of their wheeling and dealing—except for the cautious little one-talent servant. Though the servant has not lost any of the master's money, he hasn't invested it to make more. "I knew that you were a harsh man, reaping where you did not sow, and gathering where you did not scatter seed; so I was afraid, and I went and hid your talent in the ground" (vv. 24-25).

It's a curious thing for the servant to say about the master. Nothing we have seen in the story suggests that the master is "a harsh man." Softhearted, soft-headed perhaps, but does squandering your entire life savings upon your servants seem "harsh" to you?

The master, who up to this point in the story seems incredibly gracious and generous goes berserk. He begins screaming, cursing the slave, yelling out financial advice, ripping the one little talent from his hands, calling him "wicked," "worthless," and ending in a crescendo of wrath, "throw him into the outer darkness, where there will be weeping and gnashing of teeth" (v. 30), one of the few places where Jesus mentions what we call "hell."

Before you condemn the master's denunciation, recall how this story began—with the master's incredible generosity. Is the parable making a connection between the incredible grace of God and the fierce accountability demanded by a gracious God?

The love of Christ does not extinguish God's gift of our freedom as human beings. And yet our refusal is cast into doubt, as if it cannot be the ultimate word on things. The "ultimate word on things" is always God's word, and not ours. Thus it is possible to believe that hell is a reality but also an absurdity that cannot be fit into the scheme of things, that is, reality as we know it in Jesus Christ. Hell is thus absurd and hard to conceive but also a possibility. Hell may exist, but it exists always in the bright light of Christ's love. In that searing light, hell becomes a strange aberration similar to our aberrant rebellion and sin. As Neuhaus says, talk of hell in the New Testament, therefore, takes on the character not of "this is what you are going to get in the end," but rather "this is what will be defeated in the end."

I've never cared for Paul's claim, in Romans 13 that we should be "subject to the governing authorities" because "there is no authority except from God, and those authorities that exist have been instituted by God" (Rom 13:1). What theological justification is there for giving such high honor to politicians? But then I noticed that Paul says that the governing authorities have been put there by God. The politicians' power is a gift from God. The politicians are lackeys for God. Put in power by God, they shall be held accountable to the God who gives them all they have. In the light of God's propensity to hold to account, Romans 13 offers little comfort to politicians.

As Jesus says, "I came not to judge the world, but to save the world. The one who rejects me and does not receive my word has a judge; on the last day the word that I have spoken will serve as judge" (John 12:47-48). Jesus is the Judge who doesn't have to be our future judge; his gracious word is our judge already.

Just as Christ was slain in order to be made alive, so we are called to participate in dying and rising. Perhaps the wrath, the just judgment of God upon us is a kind of slaying, a kind of baptismal death to our illusions and lies, that pain that happens when we are given time to stare into the mirror of truth, the pain that is harsh but also is due to love?

PURGATORY FOR PROTESTANTS?

Here it seems is a possible Protestant argument in behalf of Catholic purgatory, the time that people are given to wait until they are better able to accept the full intimacy of God that is heaven. In our sin and rebellion, we cannot bear to look at the true face of God. And yet, if we are brought to the truth about ourselves before God, then we are ready to be with God. "We will be like him, for we will see him as he is" (1 John 3:2). If judgment is to be made to stare in the fierce, merciful mirror of truth, and if we turn away from that truth, might God allow us yet more time to turn around and look in the mirror? If so, I think that's what the church meant when it spoke of purgatory. Jesus says the shepherd searches for the lost sheep, the woman seeks the lost coin, the father waits *until.* . . . That "until" may be one of the most comforting words in all of Scripture. How long is "until"? Presumably, if God is eternal, "until" means forever, as long as it takes. The idea of purgatory is an affirmation of the possibility that Jesus seeks us in order to save us, seeking us as long as it takes, seeking us not only in life but also in death. Remember, Jesus Christ is "Lord of both the dead and the living" (Rom 14:7-9).[10] C. S. Lewis said that whenever he gets to heaven he fully expects to stand before God and, in a grand moment of recognition, he will exclaim, "So, it was *you* all along. Everyone I ever loved, it was you. Everything decent or fine that ever happened to me, everything that made me reach out and try to be better, it was you all along."[11]

Timing is important. Samuel Beckett called time, "That double-headed monster of damnation and salvation."[12] We delude ourselves into thinking that there will always be more time; only to be graced by God with enough time to come to God. As a Wesleyan, I want to be sure that we keep sanctification (what God does in us) tied to justification (what God does for us). In Christ we may hope not only for forgiveness but, by God's grace, for change.

Some years ago I was urged to be a candidate for the presidency of a college. Having spent two decades in higher education as professor, trustee, administrator, fundraiser, and critic, I was convinced by friends that I was the person for the job. During my interview, I told them that I was sure that God had prepared me for the tasks ahead, and I presented documents that stated the value that I could bring to the leadership of the college.

To my surprise, the acting chair of the search committee left a message on my answering machine some weeks later telling me that the committee had decided that I wasn't right for the job. I was humiliated. I brooded.

Some time later, I encountered a member of the search committee in the airport. We happened to be on the same delayed flight and thus were thrown together for a few painful hours of waiting. It was awkward. We kept our conversation on vague generalities of this and that. Then without my asking, he brought up the college's presidential search that had occurred a year before.

"I'm surprised that you were surprised not to be chosen. Your clergy friends worked against you. Who better knows you than your fellow clergy? You came across as intimidating in the interview, like you were going to change things at the college. We didn't think our faculty could handle that. They are provincial. The college was fearful of change and innovation."

I was stunned. But also oddly reassured. I thought that this man bore some sort of animus toward me—I certainly bore animus toward him. Despite what I had thought, the decision had been made on the basis of a host of factors, many of which had nothing to do with me, some of them having to do with an honest (if, it seems to me, misguided) assessment of the college. I realized that I would have had real difficulty trying to lead there with my misaligned expectations. The fruit of that hour-long conversation was reunion. I felt fully reconciled to this man. I repented of my earlier anger toward him. I was at peace. I gave thanks to God for the gift of our conversation that had led to my transformation.

Was it only fate or happenstance that brought us together for that extended airport conversation? Or was it the providential hand of God? What if God uses any life after this life, in an even more intense way, for some of the same transformative activity that God has been engaged in during this life? What if Origen is right that hell is the purgatorial gift of time, time to be reconciled, to have the time to face the truth about ourselves and time to heal the rifts between us? What if eternal life turns out to be something like being trapped in an airport waiting lounge with all those whom you have wronged, and who have wronged you, and all the time in the world to work it out?

Does that sound like heaven to you, or hell? Perhaps a major difference between heaven and hell is the difference in how we use the time, how God uses us in the meantime. In salvation, God takes time. God makes our time God's time. Is there a point in which God says, "Time's up for you. You had your time and you blew it"?

I don't know. I do recall the parable of the farmer and the unproductive, unresponsive fig tree. Is the pleading servant Jesus? Is our present time—in which we are pruned, weeded, and cultivated, along with lots of manure piled upon us—a gracious divine gift of forbearance? Does God's patient forbearance have limits? All I know for sure is that the One who told that story was crucified by us and still God did not call time on us. When he pronounced, even in agony on the cross, "Father, forgive them; for they do not know what they are doing" (Luke 23:34), perhaps the forgiveness was the gift of time to figure out what we're doing.

Revelation says that, at the end of time even "the kings of the earth," those most vile of all men who stood with the beast and the false prophet, will be invited to enter New Jerusalem (Rev 19:19). It is curious to see these vile politicos trotting into paradise considering that Revelation also maintains that "Outside are the . . . fornicators and murderers . . . everyone who loves and practices falsehood" (22:15), "nothing unclean will enter" (21:27). Outside the gates is nothing except the lake of fire, so the way I figure it God must have done some purgatorial work among this crowd of kings and murderers in the meantime that now makes them ready to take up residence in New Jerusalem. The great P. T. Forsyth speculated, "There are more conversions on the other side than on this."[13]

Recently a number of my churches spent a couple of months conducting a "Celebrate Recovery" program. I know that many United Methodists are addicted to various substances, but isn't church more than a sanctified twelve-step program? As tough as recovery can be, it should be noted that Christians hope for more than recovery. Our hope is for the time to receive nothing less than salvation. Standing at the edge of an open grave, I intoned from the liturgy that we stood there, "in sure and certain hope of the resurrection of the dead." We have that sort of hope for our salvation, written by God over every dead end, "To be continued."

In "The Mower," Philip Larkin ends his poem on the brevity of life by saying "we should be kind, / While there is still time." How true. Human love is made all the more precious because human life is finite. Enjoy this love now, for we shall end. But perhaps divine love is dearer because it is infinite. We should come to terms with the God who is determined to come to terms with us, now. We should learn to love this God, now, for there is, by God's grace, time.

Christianity is a kind of school in which we, sometimes momentously and dramatically, more often gradually and progressively, learn to see the God who was once regarded as our judge and enemy as none other than our savior and friend. The dependence we feared becomes friendship embraced. Such recognition requires more time for some than for others.

Scripture indicates not only that God is for us but also that God takes time for us. Herein is our hope for salvation.

The paradigmatic salvation story in the Old Testament is the exodus when God dramatically delivers the Hebrew slaves from the grip of the Empire. What was God doing during the 430 years while the Hebrews languished in bondage? We who love instant everything are amazed that God's salvation takes so long. How long is a long time for the process of what God wants to do with us? God takes time.

IN THE END, REDEMPTION

In a sermon I once said something inane like "good things do not always happen to good people and bad things do not always happen to bad people" (such was the level of my profundity then). That next week a professor in my congregation told me a story:

"Last week I attended the funeral of a man whom I've known since high school. He was always a good-looking, athletic sort of guy. The girls adored him, and he returned the favor. I envied his womanizing when we were in high school. We went to college together. He played tennis, studied little, got by in his grades, took advantage of a number of women along the way. Drank a great deal. I hadn't much contact with him since college, other than periodic reports of the end of this or that marriage, and the beginning of another new one. In the end, his liver got him at fifty. My mother called me when he died and thought it would be kind of me to go to his funeral. I stood beside the grave with some anonymous woman, a preacher, and the undertaker. His children refused attendance. He was broke and alone when he died. My point is that most of the time bad things do not happen to bad people; *but sometimes they do*. We reap what we sow. God is not forever mocked."

Though hell is tough to reconcile with our belief in a resourceful, loving God, Hell is an eternally possible impossibility. As Jesus says, "for God all things are possible" even the eternal punishment of rich people like me and you (Matt 19:26). Again, recall 1 Timothy 2:4: God "desires everyone to be saved and come to the knowledge of the truth." In 1 Corinthians 15:28, Paul asks us to look forward to the time "when all things are subjected to him . . . that God may be all in all." Some translations have the "all" as "everything to everyone."

To be converted is to be alive to this promise, indeed to live by and for this promise now. That is how Catherine of Siena could say, "All the way to heaven is heaven, because he said 'I am the way.'" Those who know Christ already know something of heaven because Christ is both the way and the destination. The risen Christ and those who run with the risen Christ are the forerunners, and their lives here, now are foretaste of the coming great banquet for all. By living in Christ and for Christ, we anticipate by faith the future redemption of all things. Again Paul:

> For the creation waits with eager longing for the revealing of the children of God . . . in hope that the creation itself will be set free from its bondage to decay and obtain the freedom of the glory of the children of God. We know that the whole creation has been groaning in labor pains until now. (Rom 8:19-22)

We have the first fruits, but as Neuhaus notes there are Christians who seem to think that we first fruits are the *only* fruits. The church is preview of the great harvest that is to be. Our job is to show the unreconciled what reconciliation looks like—a somber thought when one considers how we Christians actually live before the world.

The hope that all may be saved, that hell may be empty, offends some Christians. For them it is as though there is only so much of God to go around, as though God's grace to others will somehow diminish our portion of grace. Remember the parable of the workers in the vineyard (Matthew 20), how those who came early in the day complained that those who arrived later got the same pay. What does the master say? "Take what belongs to you, and go; I choose to give to this last as I give to you. Am I not allowed to do what I choose with what belongs to me? Or are you envious because I am generous?" And then Jesus adds, "So the last will be first, and the first will be last" (vv. 14-16).

Neuhaus says he has actually heard the objection, "What's the point of being a Christian if, in the end, everyone is saved?" He answers: What's the point of being first rather than last in serving the Lord of love? Why be found rather than lost? Why know the truth rather than living in ignorance? What's the point? To ask the question is to have missed the point.

So even though it may be possible that many will be eternally damned, it's hard to square that with the Bible's depiction of a God who searches "until" he finds. If hell is a place of eternal torment for the damned, then heaven must be a place of eternal sadness for the blessed and hasn't Revelation 21:4 promised that one day God will "wipe away every tear from their eyes"?

There are Christians who have argued to the contrary. They say if we pray "thy will be done" then we should rejoice at God's willful condemnation of the damned. Some medieval theologians said that one of the attractions of heaven is the pleasure that the saved will have in watching the torments of the damned.

To hope that hell is empty, that Christ has at last fully got that for which he so suffered, is of course, to hope implicitly for our own salvation. Only God knows our final destiny. This is not cause for discouragement or paralyzing insecurity. It is a basis of our faith. In my experience, most folk who are confident that hell is packed and have a list of hell's inhabitants are supremely confident of their own salvation. To those who were a little too sure of having their ticket to salvation, Paul declares, "work out your own salvation with fear and trembling" (Phil 2:12—a statement dearly loved by John Wesley). But then, lest we be overcome by fear and trembling, Paul immediately adds, "for it is God who is at work in you, enabling you both to will and to work for his good pleasure" (Phil 2:13—a statement that Wesley loved even more).

George W. Bush, newly born-again, got into an argument with Mom Bush over just who would be in heaven. "Bush maintained that only born-again Christians were eligible for entrance. . . . Barbara Bush disagreed and telephoned [Billy] Graham to let him settle the matter. The evangelist said that while the younger Bush's reading of the Bible might be technically correct, he warned both of them that no one should try to play God—for God alone knows who has or has not received Christ as their Savior."[14]

Paul says that even he does not know how he will fare at the final judgment. Our earnest hope is that someday, by the utterly undeserved grace of God, we will hear the words Jesus graciously spoke to the thief, "Today you will be with me in Paradise" (Luke 23:43). The Bible's words of warning and promise should lead each of us to repentance, as words addressed to *me*. Curiosity about what will happen to others could be idle distraction. Besides, "Salvation belongs to our God who is seated on the throne, and to the Lamb!" (Rev 7:9-10).

As the Letter to the Hebrews puts it, "Now faith is the assurance of things hoped for, the conviction of things not seen" (11:1). "Assurance" means conviction, confidence, trust. Faith as hope is confidence in God's faithfulness lived in the light of God's salvation in Christ. The gospel of Jesus Christ, and the abundant mercy we find there, undermines our cocksureness to the point that, although we know what we sinners deserve, we are less sure, because of his love, of what we shall actually receive.

Here's the way Richard Neuhaus puts it:

> When I come before the judgment throne, I will plead the promise of God in the shed blood of Jesus Christ. I will not plead any work that I have done, although I will thank God that he has enabled me to do some good. I will plead no merits other than the merits of Christ. . . . I will give everlasting thanks. I will not plead that I had faith, for sometimes I was unsure of my faith, and in any event that would be to turn faith into a meritorious work of my own. I will not plead that I held the correct understanding of "justification by faith alone," although I will thank God that he led me to know ever more fully the great truth. . . . Whatever little growth in holiness I have experienced, whatever strength I have received from the company of the saints, whatever understanding I have attained of God and his ways—these and all other gifts received I will bring gratefully to the throne.[15]

The Crucifixion is therefore the most luminous revelation of what God does. "Now is the judgment of this world; now the ruler of this world will be driven out. And I, when I am lifted up from the earth, will draw all people to myself" (John 12:31-32). When we stand and affirm, "I believe in God the Father Almighty," this is the "almightiness" that we are affirming. We have been enlisted in the first act of a drama that is presented in our churches on Sunday, but shall one day, in eternity, be forever.

To believe that is to judge the church for its timidity and dullness that inadequately shows the world the glory that awaits. And yet we believe that one day there is hope that the great curtain shall be raised. "All flesh shall see it together"—the glory of the Lord, the great panoramic vision of a world redeemed and restored, a creation healed. And if we happen to be standing near those who are seeing that vision for the first time, the vision that we have only seen in glimpses on Sunday morning, we will be able to explain, "See? This was what we were trying to sing and to say, what we were trying to show you all along through the church's pitiful attempts at proclamation. This is that great feast that we were only beginning, in a modest way in the church, but now we shall all enjoy together forever!"

> I pray that you may have the power to comprehend, with all the saints, what is the breadth and length and height and depth, and to know the love of Christ that surpasses knowledge, so that you may be filled with all the fullness of God. Now to him who by the power at work within us is able to accomplish abundantly far more than all we can ask or imagine, to him be glory in the church and in Christ Jesus to all generations, forever and ever. Amen. (Eph 3:18-21)

A couple of weeks ago I went to a funeral of one of the true saints of the church. In the sermon, her pastor praised her for all the good that she had done over the years, in her church and in her community. He enumerated the lives that she had touched. He praised her as an exemplar of Christian virtues.

A week later I went to another funeral. The deceased had made a string of errors in life. Throughout adulthood he struggled with an addiction to alcohol. He had never been able to hold a job. His addiction combined with his bitter personality, made his children's lives, and his wife's life, rather miserable. In the end, he stuck the barrel of a shotgun in his mouth while in a drunken stupor and pulled the trigger.

At this funeral, the pastor began his sermon by saying, "Jerry was always troubled, from the first. We found out this week that he was even more troubled than any of us feared. Jerry made a mess of just about everything he touched. He disappointed people he loved, and he kept messing up. I really liked Jerry, but today, I'm so mad at him I can hardly stand it.

"But this is the church, and we have not come to focus upon Jerry's mistakes, but rather we have come to focus upon the work of the God who loved Jerry even in his mistakes. Can we worship, even in the face of this tragedy? Yes we can! The same God who created Jerry saw him every day of his life. The God who gave Jerry life, looked at him even more graciously than the most generous of us. We know from Scripture that our Savior has a place in his heart for the people who mess up. He promised us that he never stops seeking us sinners. He continues to reach out to Jerry today. I wonder if Jerry is even now being embraced by the God who loved him and who would do anything for him. Right after Jesus says, 'Jerry, I'm so mad at you I can hardly stand it,' he will say, 'Still, you are a sheep of my fold, a lamb after my own heart. Welcome.'"

Note that the pastor was forced, by the circumstances of this man's life, to focus, at the end, not upon this man's life, but on the nature and the work of God in Jesus Christ. In the end, that is the only hope for us all in life, in death, in any life beyond death.

In so much of mainline Protestantism, we splash in a shallow pool. We offer moralistic admonition, advice, and encouragement, but many times it's not much different than people could hear anywhere else. Most of us pastors relate to people who are not too troubled, not too messed up, not too great failures at life. But what do you say when people come to a dead end, a brick wall, when there is no hope for human work or human progress? In extremis, at the end, we are forced to offer more than therapy.

That's when we are pushed toward cosmic, end-of-time talk like the Revelation or 1 Thessalonians. We dare to speak about heavenly ends. Christ becomes more than personal. We proclaim a God who triumphs cosmically, a God who isn't stumped by our sin and our rebellion, a God who is relentlessly redemptive, a God who acts not just for me but for all.

As a preacher (someone who, on a weekly basis, prances about the chancel pronouncing, "Thus saith the Lord . . .") I, especially I, can tell you that if Jesus Christ doesn't love sinners enough to reach out and save sinners, I'll be damned.

CHAPTER SIX

WHAT ABOUT THEM?

A friend and I entered a dingy diner in rural South Carolina at lunch-time. Nothing but pickups were parked out front. At nearly every table sat working people, almost all of them wearing baseball caps, having lunch. Almost every table seemed equally divided racially, white and black. There was much laughter and conviviality. My friend, surveying the scene said, "We've walked in to the kingdom of God."

Then he said, "Don't you wonder what this crowd talked about at lunch the day after the O. J. Simpson verdict?"

In racially divided America, a racially inclusive diner is a glimpse of the hope that moves us. Here is church as it's meant to be—that gathering convened by God where we are forced to be in conversation with those whom we might have avoided had not God brought us together. To be sure, the kingdom of God is more than a bunch of diverse people having a meal together. But Christians believe that although just eating together and talking about difficult subjects is not the end of the Kingdom, it could well be its beginning. That's what we do every Sunday. When Christians enact and celebrate salvation in Jesus Christ, we do it with a meal, the Eucharist. This holy meal preserves salvation from being intellectualized by us, made a matter of our feelings, our decisions, our projects. Salvation is when we come to the table, with those we may not necessarily like, and we hold out empty hands, receive a gift, obeying Jesus' command, we "do this" rather than think about it, we share, we ingest, and Jesus becomes our life.

Of course, neither I nor my friend would know any of this without Jesus. Jesus teaches what kingdom of God designates, Jesus who first implants in us the hope that there is such a time and place that is our destiny, Jesus who is host at the table, Jesus who trains us to bend our lives toward this hope rather than any other.

Salvation is literally inconceivable apart from Christ: "There is salvation in no one else, for there is no other name under heaven given among mortals by which we must be saved" (Acts 4:12). Peter wasn't speaking to the question of other faiths—he was testifying before his fellow Jews about the Jew, Jesus. Still Peter's statement does represent what the church has always and everywhere believed about the name of Jesus. If Jesus is, as we believe him to be, as much of God as we ever hope to see, the one who uniquely brought about our *at-one-ment* with the Father, then we can't also say that Jesus is only a way, one truth among many, and just another life. Jesus is not simply a great moral example; he is the salvation of God, God's peculiar, unsubstitutable fullness. Jesus' distinctive way of suffering, sacrificial love, outrageous invitation, and boundary-breaking, government-enraging, relentless seeking—vindicated by surprising, unexpected resurrection—cannot be merged with other means or definitions of salvation.

If, in the mercy and mystery of God, people might be saved who have never even heard of Christ, never got their invitation to his table, we believe that they are still saved *because* of Christ, because Jesus' way of suffering, sacrificial love, vindicated by surprising, convivial resurrection is the way that enables God to show kindness to the good and the bad, the just and the unjust, the knowing and the unknowing, for "there is salvation in no one else" (Acts 4:12).

Some Christians are discomfited by this claim. Richard Neuhaus says that they are intimidated by an anti-intellectual culture that decrees that all truths are equal. Who are you to claim that you have truth and others do not? Why is Christ, as the Truth, any more adequate than any other truth? I've known some wonderful people who were atheists. What does it matter what you believe as long as you are sincere and try to be a good person? What is truth other than what works for you? And so on and so on.

I reassert what was said at the beginning: our salvation is not ours to *have*, as if this were a possession under our control. Salvation is an invitation we have received. Here is peculiar Truth who tells us things we don't want to hear, who makes demands upon us we would not have made upon ourselves, Truth that often works against us as much as for us, who thereby offers us a gift we do not deserve. Jesus' most severe criticism was of his own followers, saying nothing negative about any other faith. Jesus saves sinners, not correct believers. Still, we must testify to what has happened to us. We ungodly have been encountered by the Truth as God in Jesus Christ and by his grace (gift). We have (despite ourselves) responded to that encounter by faith. Our worlds have been dramatically changed, though none of us have responded as fully as we ought. We hope and pray and work for everyone to be so encountered and fully to respond because Jesus has made the unsaved our assignment.

Barth said the main difference between a Christian and a non-Christian is "noetic," a difference of what is known. Christians are not more moral than non-Christians. Non-Christians, for Barth, live as those who are "designated Christians"; what Jesus Christ has done for the world, he has done for them, though they have not yet heard his call, have yet to know his election of them as his disciples.

The believer, by the grace of God, knows something that the nonbeliever does not yet know. Both the believer and the nonbeliever are living lives that are bounded by grace, living in a world radically determined by what happened in the cross and resurrection of Jesus. Barth says that "our real distinction from non-Christians will consist in the fact that we know that Jesus Christ himself, and he alone, is our hope as well as theirs, that he died and rose again for those who are wholly or partially non-Christians, that his overruling work precedes and follows all being and occurrence in our sphere, that he alone is the perfect Christian, but that he really is this, and it is in our place."[1]

Knowing what we know, we have expectation that someday,

> at the name of Jesus
> every knee should bend,
> in heaven and on earth and under the earth,
> and every tongue should confess
> that Jesus Christ is Lord,
> to the glory of God the Father. (Phil 2:10-11)

Although I see Barth's point, as a Wesleyan, I believe that being a Christian is much more than the intellectual, noetic matter of knowing something. We don't only know something; we know Someone who speaks, reveals, demands, commands, who not only reveals but also prods, commissions—well, you get the point. Salvation is not only about God's work in Jesus Christ but also about God's work in us. Salvation and human transformation go hand in hand. God's grace working in us makes a Christian different from the non-Christian in ways that are beyond the noetic.

Even though other faiths are not a major biblical concern, the question has been pressed upon the church, such as during the period of Islamic conquest in the Middle Ages or today when our best friend is a Buddhist. The question has become a large concern in our age for secular political reasons rather than specifically Christian theological ones. I don't hear too many Christians who are troubled that they are not doing all they ought to witness to those of other faiths. The question is usually posed by people who are worried about how we are to maintain a unified, democratic nation with so much diversity and so little intellectual equipment to handle true difference.

The modern world has convinced itself that differences in religion are terribly dangerous, the source of great conflict and peril. This is one of the mechanisms whereby the modern state deflects attention from itself as the main source of death and mayhem. The modern world has a tendency toward enforced unity and suppression of difference because the state tolerates no serious competitors to its sovereignty. Most of what the modern state calls *united* is the result of various forms of coercion—legislative, military, or simply that fostered by effective advertising.

Postmodernity is learning to admit to the reality and persistence, even the blessing of difference, though differences in religion are still suspect. The church has, through most of its history, lived with the fact that there are those—often a majority—who disagree with our view of reality and assert a counterview. Christianity has had fierce resistance to its truth claims from every culture in which it found itself, including the very first cultures in which we found ourselves. Other faiths are simply what the Bible calls "other gods" or, not too charitably, "false gods" and the people who follow these faiths are "Gentiles." I shall discuss other faiths as a sort of practical implication of salvation. Remember that I speak as a kind of honorary Jew, as one who was (still is) what Scripture would call a "Gentile" and who is therefore still shocked that the promises of God, spoken only to Israel, somehow got extended even to me. When Paul is rejected after speaking in the synagogue at Antioch, he says that he now turns "to the Gentiles," citing Isaiah 49:6 as precedent, "I will give you as a light to the [Gentiles], that my salvation may reach to the end of the earth" (Acts 13:47). This suggests that much of the New Testament—certainly the Acts of the Apostles—is an attempt to explain the oddity of how the salvation of Israel is now offered even to the Gentiles, that is, *to us.* Our Gentile salvation requires the most belabored Pauline theological explanation. For us Johnny-come-latelies to treat salvation as our achievement, our Gentile possession, is sick. In talking about other faiths, we are talking about our kin.

One of Paul's stunning theological discoveries was that God is not only God of Jews but also of Gentiles (Rom 3:20). Presumably Paul might say that God is God of Jews and Gentiles, that is, Muslims and Buddhists too.

Paul did not move toward the Gentiles from some mushy theory of plu-ralism but rather because of what he had personally experienced of God in Jesus Christ. God's revelation in Jesus Christ was particular, singular, de-cisive, and unique, and Paul's expansive view of God was based upon a call by the inclusive Christ rather than despite an exclusive Christ. As we have noted, Acts says that this was the reason for Paul's "conversion" on the Damascus road—so that he might announce salvation to the Gentiles (Acts 9:15).

Paul had an ethical corollary to his soteriology—we ought to welcome others as Christ has welcomed us (Rom 15:7; Gal 3:28). An inclusive, hos-pitable, pluralistic church keeps closely tied to the Jesus who welcomed and who died for all sinners. Strange that in our time, in the minds of many, the notion that the name of Jesus Christ saves, that which moti-vated Christians to move out into all the world in mission, should be re-garded as that which gives Christians reasons for excluding others ("We're saved, sorry about you") or for the cessation of mission ("We mustn't at-tempt to evangelize others because that implies that we arrogantly think we are right and they are wrong").

Paul's prime example of the fully justified, righteous believer is Abra-ham (Romans 4), a man who had never heard of Jesus. Somehow, what Jesus did, he did even for Abraham who knew nothing of what Jesus did. Still, if anyone is saved without knowing about Jesus, that person's salva-tion is still an event that occurs through Jesus, as Paul might put it. And if Abraham could be saved, having never heard of nor confessed faith in Jesus, then it is not too great a leap to believe that someone who has never heard about Jesus might be similarly saved. When Peter baptized the Roman S.S. Officer (I mean Centurian) Cornelius, Peter explained that through revelation from Jesus he now saw that God shows "no partiality" and that anyone who fears God, in any nation, and does what is right is acceptable to God (Acts 10:34). God has acted uniquely, but not exclusively to save in Jesus Christ. There is something about salvation *in the name of Jesus Christ* that blurs boundaries and creates capacity, nurturing generosity to those in other religions.

Salvation is only one of the words that we must explain, define, ex-emplify, and unpack for the uninitiated. When Christians say "salvation," we are not simply applying our word to what Hindus call deliverance (*mok-sha*) or Buddhists call release (*nirvana*). We are talking about something else. We are talking about participation in the generous reign that Jesus Christ proclaimed. Salvation is when we take our place in that promised sovereignty. And when you are following a crucified Savior, his reign, his salvation can seem to the outside observer as something less than the popular conception of salvation. As we have said, salvation's content is determined by the specific narratives of Jesus Christ. Those stories render the strange new world that is salvation. So it doesn't make much intellectual sense for someone to claim that Buddhists are *saved* in the same sense that Christians use the word because when a Buddhist thinks *save* the Buddhist is talking about something different from what Christians mean by salvation.

Having said this, we ought also to note that as Christians we are unsurprised to discover God at work in other religions. Our guiding narrative tells a story of one God whose love is comprehensive, all embracing, inclusive, and cosmic. Our stories speak of the shock that God's people experienced when they find God working, not just among us good Torah-believing Jews, but also across the street, among *them*. A great part of the tension in the New Testament comes from the church (Jewish and Gentile Christians) awakening to the discovery that God has a considerably larger notion of family. At least one of the major reasons why Jesus was crucified was for telling all us righteous ones that, "the tax collectors and the prostitutes are going into the kingdom of God ahead of you" (Matt 21:31). Though I don't know many Buddhists personally, surely there are enough Buddhist whores and government lackeys to make Matthew 21:31 an important text for interesting interfaith conversation.

JESUS THE ONLY WAY?

Jesus tells his disciples that he is the way. His way is the way, that is, the same way that Jesus is walking (the way of the cross) is to be their way too. "Way" (*hodos*) is used only here in John (John 14:1). It's the same term for the Christian movement in Acts 9:2 and 22:4. It can mean not only a road, a path, but also a practice. John's Gospel ends with Jesus telling Peter, "Follow me" (21:19). Elsewhere Jesus used the metaphor of a path to speak of his own movement from God and to God. Now the path becomes a highway whereby Jesus' disciples get to God.

At last Jesus, who has been rather elusive in John's Gospel, comes forward, looks his followers in the eye, and openly declares that he is the way. "I am." His declaration is graciously simple and absolute. "I am." He doesn't say that his philosophy is the way (as Plato might have said) but rather "I am the way." A person, rather than a doctrine or a belief, is the way. It's similar to what he says elsewhere about being the "gate" and the "good shepherd" (10:7, 11), a saying much like Matthew 7:13. Because Jesus is uniquely related to the Father, he is our way to the Father. John 14:7 is a statement about destination. When we see Jesus, we see the Father. To know Christ is at last to see God.

Much of modern theology, particularly in its liberal, progressive guises, is in the grip of a counterfeit modesty. "God? God is too grand, too ethereal; therefore, it is impossible to say anything definitive about God." We wish. If God were not incarnate in Christ, then we could make "God" mean whatever we please. John 14:1 dares to assert that the one standing before us—this Jew who is soon to be crucified by an unholy alliance of church and state because of what he said and what he did—loved us enough not to be nebulous or coy. He is not just our light but also the light that enlightens the whole world. Belief in Jesus is not something added on to a belief in God, but rather belief in Jesus is our belief in God. Here, standing before us is the not only the "way" to but also the "truth" about God.

"Do not let your hearts be troubled. Believe in God, believe also in me" (John 14:1).

Troubled about what? This is a favorite verse from the Gospel for funerals, and well it should be, for it speaks words of reassurance to our troubled hearts. Let's say that "troubled" here means trouble between us and God. Where do we finally stand with God, when all is said and done? At the end, are we destined for oblivion or for communion? Christ speaks

> In my Father's house there are many dwelling places. If it were not so, would I have told you that I go to prepare a place for you? And if I go and prepare a place for you, I will come again and will take you to myself, so that where I am, there you may be also. (John 14:2-3)

"My Father's house" is an expansive edifice, with lots of room, many different places in which to dwell. It is not a small but a capacious place, with room even for disciples who betray their Master. How could Christ say that he is going to "prepare a place for you," to make even more room for us, if the Father has a small house? The Father (the expansive sower of seed, the generous employer, the sun that shines on the good and the bad) doesn't do downsize. Note also that Christ is going to prepare for us a "dwelling place," a place to abide and be with the Father at rest, as a guest.

"I will come again and will take you to myself, so that where I am, there you may be also" (14:3).

Christ is not simply going to prepare a commodious place where his followers will eventually end up. He promises to return, actively to seek them, to find them and bring them to that gracious habitation.

"Thomas said to him, 'Lord, we do not know where you are going. How can we know the way?'" (14:5).

Thomas confesses his ignorance of the way home. Disciples are utterly dependent upon the Christ to show them to the "Father's house." Then Jesus says, majestically and reassuringly,

"I am the way, and the truth, and the life. No one comes to the Father except through me" (14:6).

It is reassuring to know that the Christ-way we are on, sometimes well, sometimes poorly, is the way that the Father is making toward us. We think that John's Gospel arises in a bitter struggle between Christ-affirming and Christ-denying Jews. We are reading the literature of a persecuted, hanging-on-by-their-fingers minority, literature that is meant to strengthen a minority in their struggle with the majority. Christ reassures those who are being persecuted for following him that he is the way. For those of us who live in a majority Christian environment to simply apply this passage to ourselves ("We have the one and only way and you don't") is to do Scripture an injustice. Followers of "the Way" who were being expelled from the synagogues (9:22) dare to proclaim that their persecuted minority way as the way.

A student preparing for teaching in an inner city school asked me, "How can I be sure that Jesus is the singular way to God? How do I know Jesus is true?"

At first I thought his question arose from his intellectual struggles with the Christian faith. Then he explained: "If one day I am going to ask a wife and kids to live with me in the ghetto while I teach the poor, it would be good for me to be sure that the God who ordered me to do this is the real thing." I believe that John 14 with its majestic assertion of Christ as the real thing was originally addressed to a Christian like that student.

There is also a good possibility that this passage from John may be meant to be inclusive rather than exclusive. In this rich, expansive Gospel, the Father's house has "many rooms" (v. 2). "House" (*oikia*) can also mean "household" or "family." Jesus is the way we are adopted into God's rapidly expanding family.

There is no way for people like us to get to the Father—but now Jesus has generously opened one (Heb 10:20). We are to read John 14:1 as saying that Jesus is the open-handed way; not that he is the only way closing off any other way. In fact, in verse 7, Jesus gives explicit reassurance of the openness of his embrace. Thomas can't figure out how to get there (v. 5). Jesus reiterates, "I am the way" (v. 6). To Philip's obtuse, "Show us the Father" (v. 8) Jesus restates, "I am in the Father." For all those earnest seekers who have longed to see God, Jesus is the way that God has made to us; he is the way that we get to God and God gets to us.

Jesus ends what we first thought to be an exclusivistic discourse with an inclusivistic bomb: "I have other sheep that do not belong to this fold" (10:16). What? You mean that we—a persecuted minority who are giving our lives to follow Jesus—are not the only "sheep" God has got? (In the prayer at a funeral of someone who is not a member of the church, this is the verse that is recalled in the *Book of Common Prayer*.)

Besides, it's wise to be more metaphorical than analytical with John's Gospel. John 14 is the extravagant poetry of love. The community that first heard these words was a group of people who were swept up in loving infatuation of Jesus. They have suffered dearly for their love. Most people in love are firmly convinced that their beloved is "the one and only" for them. The one who is light to them is light to the whole world. The language is passionate and personal, centered not on a set of doctrines or beliefs, but rather on a person, a Savior who is the Beloved.

In saying that Christ is the one and only way for them, is this community also claiming that Christ is the one and only way for all? Probably, but not necessarily. On the basis of our daily experience of walking with Jesus, we Christians have difficulty imagining any other way for people like us—inherently selfish, violent, idolatrous cowards that we are—to get abundant life other than through a crucified and risen Savior like Jesus. But why should we try to imagine other possible ways, truths, and lives? We've got our hands full just trying to keep up with Jesus. Cannot we joyfully, lovingly testify to the unique, unsubstitutable way that has led us to abundant life?

I'm not advocating the generic inclusiveness or pluralism that plague much of our theology. I'm saying that if we believe that Jesus is the way, the truth, and the life, it is because Christ has lovingly made a way to us. He has come out, in the Incarnation, to love us, and it will cost him dearly (John 1:10-11). Furthermore, Christ himself says that his "way" is wide, eager, and resourceful—lots of rooms, other sheep not yet within the fold, more concern for the lost than the found, and on and on. Having found us wretched sinners, Christ says that he is determined to seek others. Unwilling to bed down with us good, faithful, middle-class "sheep," he is on the move toward "other sheep" whom "I must bring . . . also, and they will listen to my voice" (John 10:16).

Is it, "No one gets to God except by my way"? Or is it, "Everyone comes to the Father through me"? He did say, "And I, when I am lifted up . . . will draw all people to myself" (John 12:32), Jesus the great magnet, drawing in everyone, the wide door swung open to all.

Jesus' way—the way of the cross—is the way. I was helping in a church center where homeless persons are being trained for possible employment. The job trainer said to the group that this was a Christian ministry to help people get off the streets and into good jobs. A homeless man stood up and began raving, "Where do you get off telling us we need jobs? Did our Lord Jesus ever have a job? Show me in the Bible where Jesus ever said, 'Get a job, get a mortgage, and buy a home!'"

Can you believe *that* way—the way of homeless, jobless Jesus—is the only way to truth and life?

C. S. Lewis spent his life trying carefully to define and advocate for orthodox theology. But an important text for Lewis was that obscure moment at the end of John's Gospel when Peter asks Christ, "What about this other disciple, what is his ultimate fate?"

Christ responds, "What [has that to do with] you? Follow me!" (21:22). Rather than to determine who's on the way and who's got the truth, we've got our hands full just trying to follow Jesus down his wide and narrow way. Let's preach that. Believe it or not, it's the only way.

The saving role of Jesus Christ is unique because he is distinctive and different, in comparison with other alleged means of salvation be they the Buddha, Muhammad, Greek philosophy, Venus, Mars, or oat bran. In general, most Christians spend little time asserting that Jesus is the unique mediator of salvation. We know that our faith in Jesus is more a matter of our being in an obedient and loving relationship with him rather than being in a "my god is better than yours" posture.

There are those who say that although Jesus is a wonderful religious leader, he is only one means whereby humanity has salvation—Christians, as followers of Jesus, have no exclusive claim upon salvation, nor does any other one religious faith. Just as many different streams flow together to form a river, so all religions are various streams that compose the big river called *religion* or *salvation* or *reality*. Different faiths are just different ways of groping toward the larger reality of something that we call "God," but no faith knows much more about that ephemeral reality than any other faith, and so on.

Some people think like this hoping thereby not to give offense to other faiths. It seems to them exclusive and even offensive for a Christian to say that "Jesus is the unique means of salvation." Note that this thinking assumes an alternative between exclusion and inclusion—one can't exclusively affirm Jesus as the unique mediator of salvation and at the same time include Buddhists, Scientologists, and so on. Salvation is so far beyond our apprehension and comprehension, that any claim to have unique access to salvation is a failure to think with intellectual breadth and depth.

At its best, this thinking, which some call pluralism because of its concern to be fair to the plurality of faiths, is an attempt to think about these matters in a gracious way. At worst, it is a failure to think about what various faiths claim for themselves. Rather than take seriously the claims and the identifying stories of the various faiths in all their peculiarity and specificity, a new faith is laid over all other faiths—faith that to us enlightened, modern people has been given a way of thinking about conflicting and diverse faiths in such a way that their delightful differences are only apparent and therefore are unimportant and insignificant. This is a favorite intellectual ploy of modernity—take a conflicted set of ideas, boil them down to some unconflicted generality, hold hands, and sing "Kum Ba Ya," and there is no problem.

Thus Marcus Borg trots out a conventional liberal metaphor:

> The enduring religions are all paths up the same mountain. Envision a mountain, broad at the bottom, narrow at the top, the peak finally disappearing into air, space, emptiness. At the bottom, the paths are farthest apart (the external forms). But as the paths lead higher, they become closer together until they converge on the mountaintop. And then, of course, they disappear. And the place to which they lead, the mountaintop is not "heaven," but "the sacred."[2]

I despise this God-as-mountain metaphor as much as the outworn sermon illustration that compares God to a huge elephant and us to a group of blind men each groping part of the elephant (be careful!)—"The elephant is like a rope," says the man who is holding the tail. "No, an elephant is like a tree," says the one who is touching the elephant's leg, and so on. Not a very flattering image of God or of us. God is neither an inert mountain nor a stolid pachyderm. God is the searching woman, the waiting father, the resourceful farmer.

For all I know, Muslims are making their way up a very different mountain. This talk of God as a mountain or an elephant seems terribly unfair to the claims of Islam and all the other religions to whom Borg is attempting to be nice. It's a rehash of the now discredited nineteenth-century, liberal attempt to deny religious differences, to explain away religious particularities (Borg's "external forms") and merge everything into an overarching, general concept like "faith" or "religion" (or Borg's even more vague, "the sacred") that is said to be more embracing than whatever specific religions claim for themselves. Usually, the person taking this approach accuses religious people of being arrogant in asserting their way as the way, their truth as the truth. The liberal thus refuses to see the arrogance within his own position that says, in effect, "Well, you're Jewish (or Hindu or pagan and so on) but that's not as important as that we're all equally ignorant of God in differing ways so that we are all basically wandering up the same mountain, sort of."

I suppose that's how we got the notion of religion in the first place. With the birth of the modern nation state—a sovereign political entity that demands total allegiance from us and the sacrifice of our children—the nation had to do something about the problem of people running around, even in the brave new modern world, who thought that there was someone more powerful than the president and a reality more real than the modern democratic nation. Different faiths had to be melded into something called faith, and differing religions—each with their own set of stories about reality and their own distinctive and formative practices—had to be merged into generic religion, which was a strange, purely personal lifestyle choice that promised to be subservient to the state in order to be allowed to exist in the allegedly free state. Thus was the department of religion born at the university.

There is a reason that many of our Founders, like Jefferson, Franklin, and Washington, were Deists—only a vague, undemanding God could be allowed to be free in a democratic nation where the people were alleged to be God. The state was thereby uncontested to be our ultimate means of security, happiness, power, immortality, or whatever good we desire, and religion was free to be itself as long as it stayed personal and private (that is, the antithesis of just about any faith I've ever heard of). This is a major reason that pluralism isn't all that pluralistic. It tends to silence and trivialize the very faiths that it is attempting to be nice to by demanding that all of them suppress their assertions about reality and merge into the liberal, intellectually totalitarian "faith" of the modern nation state. Rather than be the source of salvation, Christianity becomes helpful in some other, officially sanctioned mode of salvation. The faith becomes personal, subjective, in order that "faith" become private and, therefore, no challenge to the dominant order.

Most Christians could tell pluralists that one of the major difficulties of worshiping and following Jesus Christ as the unique means whereby we are saved is the universal reach of his scandalously inclusive love and work. When we think "Jesus Christ" we think reach, embrace, and inclusion because that's what the Scriptures tell us about him and that's how we've experienced him in our lives. If he can reach for me—an inherently violent, narrow-minded, racist person from South Carolina—reaching toward a nice person like the Muslim who lives down the street from me is not much of a reach. To say "in Christ God was reconciling the world" (2 Cor 5:19) is to make the most inclusive of statements. Christians are able to love and to respect Buddhists as uniquely Buddhist, precisely because we are followers of the unique mediator of salvation, Jesus Christ. The internal logic of Christian theology gives us our best hope for fruitful relationships with other faiths.

At least someone like John Hick (*The Myth of God Incarnate*, 1971) has the intellectual honesty to admit that his beef with Christianity is not so much that it is arrogant and narrow, but rather that it worships the wrong God. There is just no way to worship the inherently incarnational Trinity without being involved in the evangelical reach of this God.

The Buddhist who says that there is no way to enlightenment except through the Eightfold Path is excluding Christians from that particular salvation, but I take no offense because the Buddhist is speaking of *salvation* in a sense that I in no way mean by my use of the word *salvation*. The Buddhist, as best I can understand him or her, hopes for an ultimate destiny in which his or her self with its restless strivings will be graciously extinguished. I, on the other hand, on the basis of the stories I've been told by Scripture, hope for a destiny in which my true self will be most fully realized, my strivings will be graciously redirected and fulfilled in a way I could not. My self will be developed and discovered in the complete embrace of the Savior who has so relentlessly reached toward me throughout this life and who, I believe, will continue to embrace me in whatever life there is in the future.

Though "eternal communion with Jesus Christ" is an answer to a question that other religions don't ask, it does explain why the question, "Will Buddhists be saved?" requires, "Of which salvation do you speak?" As a Christian I can understand why the Buddhist down the street hears me talk about *salvation* and responds, "Why would I want that?" After all, *I* did not want this sort of salvation, at least not at the first. I had to be enticed into it gradually, or jerked into it suddenly, over the course of a life. I didn't know, not at the first, that communion with the crucified and risen Christ was what I most wanted. I didn't know that God was preparing me for that sort of intimacy, transforming me so that I would be ready to participate in full friendship with Christ in the great house with many rooms.

THE OTHER AS GIFT OF GOD

Nothing is any more infuriating, in a conversation about religious differences, than to be told in effect, "You really agree with me, though you are not yet bright enough to see that we, after all, agree, if you just knew how to describe your faith as I have learned to describe it." Or "Christianity is mainly about loving your neighbor as yourself and, after all, don't you believe that too?" This is grossly unfair to Christianity and an indignity to foist upon disbelievers.

True dialogue begins in recognition that we are not basically "saying the same thing." If there were no genuine difference, no truly other, why talk in the first place? The demand that one relinquish any claim to significant, genuine difference is the height of intolerance.

We don't know everything, but we know enough to live and to speak with confidence, to trust the ultimate triumph of God based upon what we know of God in Christ. John Calvin said that "we shall possess a right definition of faith if we call it a firm and certain knowledge of God's benevolence towards us, founded upon the truth of the freely given promise in Christ, both revealed to our minds and sealed upon our hearts through the Holy Spirit."[3] The same one in whom we have faith is the one who was sent to the cross, in great part, because of the expansiveness of his benevolent invitation to his table. We are not superior to those to whom we give the invitation, "come and see" (John 1:46); in truth, to say to our neighbor "come and see" is to be in close solidarity with our neighbor, seeing our neighbor as our brother or sister in Christ.

Christians believe that Christ is the One toward whom all truthful accounts of the world, all true stories point, even if they do not point to him by name. Christians cannot avoid witnessing to what we believe God has worked in Christ. The error of past Christian triumphalism was not when it asserted that Jesus was the way, the truth, and the life but rather when our triumphalism forgot that it is a crucified Savior who is triumphant and we, by our smug disrespect and imperialism, deny Christ.

Jesus puts us in conversation with adherents to other faiths, not in the hope of gaining one more recruit but in order to be more fully attuned with the constant reach of Christ, in order to risk receiving correction and judgment from the person of another faith, in order to discover again the oddness and the wonder of Christ, perhaps even to witness Christ's move upon another life. Our transformation into Christ is ongoing and one way that the risen Christ gets to us is in dialogue with those who do not yet know the risen Christ.

Just before Holy Week, the rabbi at Duke casually said to me, "This is a painful week for Jews, considering our history with Christians. This week was a favorite time for the most horrific of pogroms."

I was stunned at the recognition that this week of the cross, which was so wonderful for me and my family, was a cause of pain and fear for the rabbi and his family.

"I've had to learn that the cross is not the symbol of evil and death that I once believed it to be," said the rabbi.

In that wisp of dialogue, I received both judgment from Christ and a new recognition of the oddness of salvation in Jesus Christ. I also pray that my friend the Jew received something from my willingness to listen to what he had to say to me, a Christian.

The great Jewish philosopher Martin Buber observed, "To the Christian the Jew is the incomprehensibly obdurate man, who declines to see what has happened; and to the Jew the Christian is the incomprehensibly daring man, who affirms in an unredeemed world that it has been accomplished."[4] Some of the most interesting questions about our faith are those we have forgotten how to ask. Even as I write this barefooted, saffron-robed Buddhist monks are good-humoredly standing up to one of the most oppressive governments of the world in Myanmar. On the basis of what we believe about Jesus as the Way, we Christians should be there standing with them.

During the Muslim Awareness Week at Duke, I was on a panel (representing all Christians everywhere) with our campus rabbi and an imam from Chicago. The imam says, "Islam is a religion of tolerance and peace. For instance, if my brother the rabbi is assaulted by an unbeliever, the prophet Muhammad teaches that I have an obligation to punish the unbeliever." The rabbi seemed somewhat reassured by this.

I muttered to myself, "I wish Jesus had said that to us. I've got people I'd love to punish. Alas, when we tried to take up the sword and to practice self-defense when the soldiers came to arrest him, Jesus cursed us with 'No more of this!' "

My brother the imam had taught me something about my own faith. We Christians might find interfaith conversation more fruitful if we acknowledged, upfront, that Jesus renders us weird.

Christ said that he came, not just for us, but "to give his life a ransom for many" (Mark 10:45). As Paul put it, "one has died for all" (2 Cor 5:14; cf. Rom 5:18). Whereas no other mediator than the crucified Jesus has reached out to us, that reaching we hope to be the destiny of all. And we, of all people, ought to have deep respect for the mystery of Christ's reaching out to humanity in a myriad of subtle, unrecognized at first, mysterious ways.

Pondering the fate of his fellow Jews, friends and family, Paul rises above theological hair-splitting and sings:

> O depth of the riches and wisdom and knowledge of God! How unsearchable are his judgments, and how insrutable his ways!
> "For who has known the mind of the Lord?" (Rom 11:33-34)

I met him his first day of the school year. He was tall, utterly white, utterly blonde, utterly Southern. I saw him walking on campus sometime later, hand in hand with a young woman who was utterly short, utterly brown, and (as I was to discover) utterly Muslim and, though once Persian, now an Ohioan. Sure enough, I got a call from his mother. "Have you met Thomas's girlfriend?" she asked. "Talk to him! They're serious!"

I called him in for a chat and eventually asked, "Thomas, tell me about Maranda." He told me that they were very much in love, that she was a wonderful person, and that they were planning to be married right after graduation.

I said, "Really? Tell me what brought you together."

He said, "We had so very much in common."

I said, "Thomas, you're from South Carolina, you're blonde, Baptist; she's Muslim, brown, and from Ohio. What in the world could you possibly have in common?"

He said, "Well, you know me—I don't drink on weekends, don't believe in casual sex, not really into the success-at-any-cost thing. She was the only girl I met who had the same values as mine." A pagan world makes strange bedfellows, figuratively speaking.

John runs to Jesus saying, "We saw this unknown, uncredentialed healer, out doing spectacular things, using your name when he is not even one of us, not one of us insiders" (see Mark 9:38-50).

And Jesus replies, in effect, "Hey, if he's not doing any real harm, then he's doing some good; if he's not against us, he's for us. Let the man alone." And this is in a rather "exclusive" gospel!

Extravagant, nonchalantly embracing Jesus gives texture and difficulty, promise and possibility to our parsimonious, "What about them?"

CHAPTER SEVEN

STRANGE SALVATION

It is now time for us to tackle one of the most important questions of the Christian faith: *How tall was Jesus?* Only once does anybody comment on the height of Jesus. In Luke 19:3, Luke says Jesus was "short in stature." I know, you always took that "short in stature" to refer to Zacchaeus. Zacchaeus, so they told you in Sunday school, was the little man who was so short that he had to climb up a sycamore tree to get a good look at Jesus parading through Jericho (Luke 19:1-10).

But what they should have told you is that, in the Greek, "he was short in stature" could apply as well to Jesus. Verse 3 can read, Zacchaeus "sought to see who Jesus was, but on account of the crowd could not, because he [Zacchaeus] was short in stature." But it could legitimately be read, Zacchaeus "sought to see who Jesus was, but could not on account of the crowd, because he [Jesus] was short in stature."

Jesus was so short Zacchaeus couldn't see the little rabbi for the crowd. In the earliest days of the church, critics mocked Christians' claim that Jesus was the Messiah saying that no real Son of God would be this short.

I'll make the call. Jesus was short, maybe as short as John Wesley. He was so short that the big man about town, rich Zacchaeus, had to climb up a tree just to get a peek at little Jesus.

Only Luke tells the story of Jesus entering Jericho, spotting sleazy chief tax collector Zacchaeus, and then inviting himself to the old reprobate's house for a party, once again, intruding. Luke is generally rough on the rich so it's odd to have Luke's as the sole report that when Jesus went to Jericho, he went to the house of a rich man.

Zacchaeus wasn't just a "tax collector"—lackey for the oppressive Romans, financier of state-sponsored terrorism against his fellow Jews—he was the *chief* tax collector. Therefore, he was not only a robber but also was rich. (Caustic Augustine said that a rich person is either a robber or the son of a robber.)

And he was the only person with whom Jesus feasted when diminutive Jesus came to Jericho. Just in case you didn't get the joke back in Luke 15 after parties were thrown for the stupid lost sheep, the worthless lost dime, and the profligate lost boy, Luke rubs our collective nose in it one more time: a dinner party with Hitler's henchman in Jericho. When we again grumbled, "He's gone to be the guest of a man who is a sinner!" Jesus responds (again), "Like I told you in Luke 15, the Son of Man came to seek and to save the lost. When are you going to admit to my strangeness?"

Back in Luke 15, the problem was "this fellow welcomes sinners and eats with them" (Luke 15:2). Here, it's, "He has gone to be the guest of . . . a sinner" (19:7). And Jesus says to us grumblers (note that it wasn't the "sinners," but the "righteous," who murmured against Jesus' chosen companions), "Today salvation has come to this house" (19:9).

Let's attempt one more definition of *salvation*. *Salvation* is whenever Jesus intrudes into your space, whenever Jesus makes your sinful table the site of his salvation feast, like he did for Zacchaeus. Zacchaeus didn't invite Jesus to dinner. Jesus invited himself. Hardly anyone in Scripture chooses Jesus or decides to be saved by him. The gospel is a story about Jesus' choice and decision for the lost. That's why we grumbled, still do. "He has gone to be the guest of a sinner!"

For all I know, Zacchaeus may have grumbled. Yet he eventually gets so carried away because Jesus has invited himself to his home that, when the glasses of Mogen David are raised, Zacchaeus toasts his short rabbinical guest with, "And just to show you how great it is for me to have an inspiring, though pint-sized holy man like you in our home, I'm going to give half of all I've got to the poor, and if it can be shown that I have defrauded anyone of anything, I'll restore it, I . . . ."

Jesus laughs sarcastically, "*If* it can be shown that you have defrauded anybody? Get real, Zach! All Jericho knows that you've stolen from *everybody*. You're a tax collector, for God's sake, *chief* tax collector, the godfather of all the defrauders of everybody!"

Then Jesus, having taken some of the wind out of Zacchaeus says, "Today salvation has come to this house. . . . For the Son of Man came to seek out and to save the lost" (Luke 19:9-10).

"Did you say, 'lost'?" Zacchaeus might have asked. "I'll admit that I've made a few financial mistakes and sometimes I got a bit carried away in the performance of my governmental duties, but 'lost'? Don't you think that's overstating things? Check out my tax return from last year and see if that looks 'lost' to you."

If Jesus has some odd notions of "salvation," he had odder ideas of "lost."

And we, the righteous, the insiders, those well-schooled in the faith, those in the theological know, hated him for it. After this little episode at the Zacchaeus estate, we righteous grumblers got organized. The next chapter of Luke finds Jesus up the road in Jerusalem. One of the things that Mel Gibson got wrong in his *The Passion of the Christ*, was that he never really shows why Jesus was crucified. Well, in case you wondered why a nice person like Jesus was put on a cross by affirming and including folk like us, let Luke tell you what Jesus did down in Jericho and you'll understand.

N. T. Wright says that Jesus was crucified because of the company he kept at the table, because he practiced wide-open, messianic hospitality.[1] Messiah was supposed to come and gather faithful Israel; Jesus came to seek and to save *the lost* of Israel.

Karl Barth described salvation as "God's condescension." Salvation is God not only reaching out but also specifically reaching down. Jesus makes friends in low places. Some of the lost don't know how lost they are until they get found. Salvation is Jesus getting down on our level, so that we might rise to his. I say again: salvation continues to be the most offensive thing Jesus does.

A friend of mine wrote a paper not long ago on the "marks of the true Wesleyan church." He came up with four "marks of the church" in the Wesleyan tradition: Eucharistic piety, expectation of full sanctification, gospel preaching, and identification with the poor.

Jesus comes to Jericho and identifies with the rich.

I was thrilled, a couple of years past when those sleazy Tyco executives were convicted and sent to the slammer for their corporate thievery. Jesus comes to Jericho and refuses to party with anyone except the folk who run Enron and WorldCom. It makes you wonder, just how low would Jesus stoop to save the lost?

A woman was telling me about the little church she serves in North Alabama. "We got one of the ugliest church buildings you ever saw," she told me. "I fear that some Sunday when there's a big wind, it will fall in on us."

"That's terrible," I said.

"Well, there are folk who won't come to a church if it looks too good. We got a church where nobody, no matter how low they are, will be uncomfortable."

"Hadn't thought about it that way," I said.

"And though there were no more than sixteen when I got there, God has given us some growth. Two weeks ago, I baptized six on profession of faith," she said proudly.

"You'll get this year's evangelism award," I said. "There's hardly a church in this conference that has grown by a third in one year."

"Trouble was, the week after I baptized those six, we lost six members," she said.

"You got six, but you lost six? Why?" I asked.

"They said they didn't want to go to church with a bunch of crack heads and their kids. So they left."

As her bishop I asked, "Did you explain to those who left that you and I have absolutely no control over whom Jesus saves? Did you tell them that we don't like some of Jesus' friends anymore than they?"

How tall was Jesus? What was his stature?

He was short, built low to the ground. He could, says Luke, stoop to the worst of them. By the time he got to Jerusalem, he didn't have far to fall, ending up between two low-down thieves, so short was he, so willing was he to get down and dirty with the lost.

Luke 19:1-10 is a salvation story. Jesus saves. But it was the way he saved, *who* he saved, that got Jesus into trouble. The most challenging thing about salvation in Jesus was Jesus. (The story reminds one a bit of Jesus at Levi's house in Luke 5:27-32. At the end of that dinner, Jesus says, "I have come to call not the righteous but sinners to repentance" [v. 32]). "So why is Jesus so focused on the unrighteous?" we righteous ask. One of the greatest challenges of the disciples of Jesus is to live salvation as he practiced it. "He too is a son of Abraham" (19:9) Jesus pronounces to the righteous. This one whom we despise, this one is identified as a "son of Abraham," one of our relatives. At Zacchaeus's table Jesus gathers the very first church.

ATONEMENT

The church has always found it difficult to do justice to the miracle of our justification by God in Jesus Christ. One way we have truncated God's work in the cross and resurrection of Christ is by limiting salvation to an exchange in which God forgives sin, my sin. By the Middle Ages, the church had made an almost exclusive link between salvation and sin. Anselm's 1098 *Cur Deus Homo* argued eloquently that Jesus' death was needed to satisfy an offended God whose honor had been violated by our sin. Our need was atonement—*at-one-ment*—with God. In order to enact salvation from sin and thereby accomplish atonement, an elaborate penitential system was devised. Here's what the church lovingly enables you to do so that you will be able to be saved from the punishment that your sin so richly deserves. The salvation that once was corporate and social was made private and personal.

Forgiveness for sin was the door to salvation but how could one be sure—no matter how active and relentless one's acts of piety—that God had really forgiven and opened the door for you? The Protestant Reformers sought to change this insecurity. Their remedy was to stress even more strongly the penal, substitutionary model of atonement—God is holy and God's holiness demands just punishment for sin. Our sin merits death and hell, and there is no way, no matter all your spiritual feats, to accumulate enough merit to balance out your accounts with God. In love, God solves this problem by sending his Son to undergo the punishment that should be ours. By his vicarious suffering and death on the cross, Jesus alone pays our bill and alone accomplishes our salvation.

The substitutionary model has become the semi-official doctrine of the Western church. If you want to see it dramatized, view Mel Gibson's *The Passion of the Christ*. In the movie, there is nothing to know about Jesus except that he suffered and died for us. We are the vicious actors or the passive spectators as Jesus suffers and dies on our behalf.

This is but one of the problems with the substitutionary atonement—salvation is separated from ethics. The substitutionary atonement sees the death and resurrection of Jesus as mostly changing things for us outside of this world, beyond this life. Salvation is a gracious act of God, accomplished in Jesus that solves the problem of the debt incurred by our sin and thus enables us to go to a better world someday. Salvation is thus construed as mainly about rescuing us for some other world.

When we sing, in Stuart K. Hine's popular hymn, "How Great Thou Art," "When Christ shall come with shout of acclamation, and take me home, what joy shall fill my heart," we are singing the sentiment partly engendered by the substitutionary atonement. This world is a vale of tears that is mostly untouched by the work of Christ, and we are here only awaiting deliverance to a better world than this wretched, sinful, enslaved place where we now stumble and for which we feel little responsibility in the present—other than to warn our fellow humans that they need to "accept Jesus Christ as your personal savior" so they too can be assured of escape from this sorry state.

Thus James Cone, a founder of the black theology movement, charged that the substitutionary atonement contributed to the perverse world in which slave owners could preach salvation to the slaves while in no way threatening the present master-slave establishment.[2] Gibson's film, following the standard line of the substitutionary atonement, portrays Jesus as a kind of helpless robot who for some odd reason happened to be tortured to death in order to fulfill some sort of divine plan.

Better, I believe, to say that Jesus was put to death for bringing the kingdom of God close in a way that threatened our comfortable alliances with the powers of evil. Zacchaeus shows that he really knows Jesus, though they have just met, when he says not, "Wonderful! Now I can go to heaven and live forever," but rather, "I'm giving half of everything I've got to the poor." His "heaven"—the world as God means it to be—began now, here. Jesus was put to death for being the Messiah that we were not expecting or even wanting.

Jesus responds, "Today salvation has come to this house." As Christians later affirmed, God would "gather up all things in [Christ], things in heaven and things on earth" (Eph 1:10). The world had slid away from the Creator's original intent—humanity divided into warring camps, people treating other people as things to be used and abused rather than as fellow children of God, the rich fashioning an elite, gated heaven on earth for themselves and the poor consigned to the hell of poverty. Now, in Christ, God was busy wrenching Creation away from the satanic "head" we were following, and (as Irenaeus put it) "recapitulating" all under the Lordship of Christ (Latin *caput*, "head").

Paul says that Christ is the "new Adam" in which the "old Adam," our progenitor, is redone, rescued, reworked, saved, and made new in Christ. All this happens in Christ, not only on the cross but also in every word and deed of his life. Not only was there recapitulation—a new government established over us and the world—but also reconstitution of Israel. As N. T. Wright has shown, Christians claimed that, in Christ, Israel was being reestablished as God's light to the nations, as God's answer to what's wrong with the world, as God's means for the world's salvation.[3] But perhaps even more amazingly, the twelve tribes were being not only gathered but also opened up to include even the pagans, the Gentiles who had no previous part in the promises of God to Israel. One would have thought that Jesus might have been careful to erect walls between the righteous and the unrighteous. No, his ministry is characterized by his embrace, as well as by his rearrangement of our ideas of righteous. Zacchaeus is also a son of Abraham.

Paul's great message was that "this salvation of God" is sweeping, embracing, cosmic, and decisive. Salvation is about not only God's response to the problem of our personal sin but also God's response to the problem of the whole, wonderful but rebellious creation. Whereas the church wisely never settled on one, official doctrine of the atonement, never fixed one explanation of the meaning of Christ's work on the cross as the only possible way to think about Christ, it's clear to me that Paul has something considerably larger in mind than some legal transaction that cancels my personal sin when he claims:

> For in him all things in heaven and on earth were created, things visible and invisible, whether thrones or dominions or rulers or powers—all things have been created through him and for him . . . and in him all things hold together. . . . For in him all the fullness of God was pleased to dwell, and through him God was pleased to reconcile to himself all things, whether on earth or in heaven, by making peace by the blood of his cross. (Col 1:16-20)

Zacchaeus catches the vision of a new heaven and a new earth and becomes one of its first fruits by redistributing his wealth. Salvation is not so much to be snatched from a rotten world, rescued from a botched creation as it is to join up in God's cosmic restoration, fulfillment, and grand reworking of creation in Jesus Christ, here, now. When many people in first-century Judea were encountered by Jesus, they didn't say simply, "At last God has done something about my personal sin so I can get my ticket to heaven," though that is implied. Rather it was as if they looked all the way back to Genesis and remembered our first primal rebellion, our first siblings, Cain and Abel, and all the rest and saw God bringing to fulfillment and restoration all that God intended then but did not get until the coming of Christ when God made "peace by the blood of his cross" (Col. 1:20).

From this sweeping perspective you see why I tire of being made to sing on Sunday this contemporary ditty:

> From the earth to the cross, my debt to pay.
> From the cross to the grave, from the grave to the sky.[4]

The claustrophobic, exclusively egocentric nature of this song is a long way from Romans 8 or Colossians 1. What sort of Christians are being formed by singing such music?

Jesus begins his ministry, in all the Gospels, by gathering disciples. See? He is reconstituting the twelve tribes of Israel. But he is doing more. He is

115

reaching out to those on the margins, even to those beyond Israel's boundaries, redefining what it truly means to be a son or daughter of Abraham. His salvation is an embrace, a vocation to join up, to participate in an invasion that presages a grand, cosmic revolution. In vocation he is raising the dead, creating the world; it's Easter and Genesis all over again.

If we are going to receive salvation, we've got to receive it from the one whom we murdered, killing him, in part, because he saved sinners like Zacchaeus. The words sear into our consciousness—"Jesus Christ of Nazareth, whom you crucified . . . God raised. . . . There is salvation in no one else" (Acts 4:10-12). Wouldn't it be so much easier for God if God had decided to save the good and the righteous, rather than us murderers? Wouldn't it have been less challenging for us if we were saved through some benign, serene therapist who murmurs sweetly, "I love you just the way you are, promise me you won't change a thing"? Salvation is when we recognize that, "while we still were sinners Christ died for us" (Rom 5:8). Salvation is also when I recognize that, wonder of wonders, Christ died also for Zacchaeus. And salvation is when we respond as Zacchaeus, "Lord, I will give." The hard part about Christian salvation is not in earning it but in receiving it as God gives—Nietzsche knew enough about Christian salvation (servile, "slave morality" he called it) to know that he wanted no part of it. Edward Gibbon blamed Christian salvation's fondness for rabble for the fall of the Roman Empire. Both knew more about salvation than many of those who believe that we are saved.

The responsive, personified, personal nature of salvation makes all the more curious the modern propensity to turn the Christian faith into an abstract essence, a plan, a set of propositions and ideas. The story is not about amorphous grace. It is about the peculiar definition of that grace received in the person and work of Jesus Christ. Scripture renders a living, breathing, demanding personality, not a set of freestanding, self-evident, abstract, allegedly biblical propositions. Yet then again, a personality with whom we are in relationship obligates us, demands that we take our place in the relationship. In Jesus, salvation and vocation are linked. The pardon and freedom of salvation carries with it a summons. Friendship is inherently demanding, which is one reason why we have so few friends. A proposition asks only our intellectual assent to what makes sense to us. An abstraction or a generality, no matter how noble, will never move us to love or to give half of all we've got to the poor.

NO SALVATION OUTSIDE THE CHURCH

Kant categorized the human condition as a search for an answer to three questions: What can I know? What ought I to do? For what may I hope?[5] When it came to hope, Kant said the shape of our hope is determinative of the way we live. In a sense, hoping precedes knowing and doing. Salvation is the name for Christian hope. What is the shape of our hope and how does that hope shape how we live?

The church is the crucible for such questions. Here I was told the stories that I could not have made up on my own, the stories that enable me to hope for an eventual consummation of God's intentions for the world. Here I, the lost, was found, discovered by the grace of God. Here I learned the first baby steps in my return toward home. Here I admitted that my fumbling, adolescent attempts to flee were ultimately doomed, and here I was shown that those whom I naturally regarded as strangers, enemies even, were in truth sisters and brothers caught like me in the divine dragnet of grace. Here, I was changed, here in church.

It is inconceivable that this salvation could have happened outside the church. *Extra ecclesiam nulla salus*, "apart from the church there is no salvation."[6] Before you dismiss this claim as the height of ecclesiastical arrogance—we're inside and you are out, sorry about you—recall what we have said about salvation. If salvation in Jesus Christ is corporate, even cosmic, then salvation is a social endeavor. We come to church to practice salvation, not only to be prepared now to live with a living, righteous, and loving God forever but also to pioneer those practices that are commensurate with what we now know of salvation in Christ. The church is more than the means of salvation, the path toward salvation; it is salvation embodied, practiced, and enjoyed. Open hospitality, confession of sin and receiving forgiveness, gifts to the poor, active seeking of those who don't yet know, and exploring ways to tell them the good news in such a way that they might hear and respond are among the practices necessitated by our soteriology.

A person comes up to me in a London fog and asks me of all people, "Can you point me the way to Victoria Station?" And even though I'm not a native, I was able to say, "Yes. Two blocks down that street, take a right, can't miss it." My knowledge of London is woefully inadequate, still I knew enough to point someone else the way through the fog. That's basically what we call *evangelism*.

The church is necessary for salvation. Church is more than the ark that rescues the righteous few leaving the wicked rabble to perish in the flood. The church is Christ's self-appointed means of enabling his loving movement on the world for the purpose of communion, that place where God also propelled egoists like us toward the neighbor, where we are taught to name strangers as family. The church is saved for the world, not out of it. The church is where the risen Christ graciously takes up room, locates, and incarnates.

We were all going around the room telling why we enjoyed being Methodists, why we dearly loved The United Methodist Church. Some liked the fellowship, others liked the friends, some liked the music.

"Part of me hates The United Methodist Church," one young woman said. "Before I became a Methodist, my life was my life. I was fairly content with myself. Then the church took me to Haiti and made me stand near people who are dying because of their dire poverty yet who were also undeniably richer in faith than I would ever be. I could have had a fairly happy life without the church. Now, those strangers in Haiti have become my obsession. I'm thinking about them as if they were my family. I've got the church to blame for that."

In the Liturgy of the Hours, Tuesday, mid-afternoon prayer, the Catholic Church prays, "Help us to work generously for the salvation of the world so that your Church may bring us and all mankind into your presence. Grant this through Jesus Christ our Lord."

Our salvation, being a gift, also implies a summons. In salvation we are enlisted by God to work with God in the salvation of the world. We begin to worry about the things that God seems to worry about. The elect are chosen for a task. Thus vocation is always an aspect of salvation. The paradigmatic instance is the call of Saul on the Damascus road (Acts 9) where Saul is dramatically encountered to be God's "chosen instrument" to bring salvation to the Gentiles. Although the church usually refers to this story as "the conversion of Saul" it is more properly "the vocation of Saul." Saul is saved, converted because God has a job for him to do.

As we noted earlier, salvation is not only God's work for us on the cross (justification) but God's continuing work in us now (sanctification); God works in us that we might work for God. John Wesley was clear that our salvation meant a linking of justification with sanctification:

> By salvation I mean, not barely (according to the vulgar notion) deliverance from hell, or going to heaven, but a present deliverance from sin,

a restoration of the soul to its primitive health, its original purity, a recovery of the divine nature, the renewal of our souls after the image of God in righteousness and true holiness, in justice, mercy, and truth. This implies all holy and heavenly tempers, and by consequence all holiness of conversation.[7]

"All this is from God," Paul writes to the Corinthians, "who reconciled us to himself through Christ, and has given us the ministry of reconciliation" (2 Cor 5:18). God "reconciled us" in order to give us "the ministry of reconciliation." "For our sake he made him to be sin who knew no sin, so that in him we might become the righteousness of God" (2 Cor 5:21).

When asked just who is saved and who isn't, Karl Barth's favorite response was to quote 2 Corinthians 5:19, "in Christ God was reconciling the world to himself." Period. But then note the following verse: "we entreat you . . . be reconciled to God." Assignment follows gift, exhortation follows fast on the heels of proclamation, human response after divine initiative. Be who you are, now that Christ has reconciled the world to God—this is my paraphrase of the gospel preached while standing on one foot. The primary, normative place for this message and its enactment is the church.

When Paul says that we in the church are ministers of reconciliation and active agents of the righteousness of God, Paul surely spoke with a touch of irony in his voice. He was writing to a congregation in a mess. Jesus was raised from the dead, defeated death and Satan, sallied forth from the tomb dragging behind him this *bride*, the poor old, compromised tart that was First Church Corinth as the first fruits of his victory. Some victory, that one. It is a victory similar to his great conquest on Good Friday at Golgotha when Jesus culminates his years of teaching and preaching, healing and prophecy, and suffering and dying with nothing to show for it but one miserable, utterly untutored, somewhat repentant thief.

If we had any modesty, the church would blush at Paul calling us the first fruits of Jesus' victory. God knows the church has found ever more perverse ways of betraying Christ and making him look foolish for calling us his very body. This grim admission is a cue for Paul once again to teach, "Christ died for the ungodly" (Rom 5:6). I guess you would have to be in the church to know why for those of us in the church, even the deep ineptitude of the church becomes an occasion for the grace of God in Christ more brightly to shine. We, the "righteousness of God."

In a discussion about the fate of his fellow Jews, Paul's major example of the power of God to save is none other than the head of the evil empire,

Pharaoh (Rom 9:17-18). Thus I am bold to hope that Jesus may find a way to save a wretch like Adolph Hitler—not because I have any affection for the old murderer, and certainly not because I hope to bump into Adolph in eternity—but because if Jesus can find a way to forgive and to save a wretch like me, well . . . I anticipate the possibility of hearing Adolph say, through tears, "I was wrong." And I look forward to seeing if I have internalized my belief that there's no salvation outside the church to the degree that I can embrace even Adolph as a brother. We'll see. Jesus has promised us lots of time to get used to the idea.

I wish the church could get better in our discipleship, could succeed in being the bride that Jesus thinks we are. Still, when the world points to the triviality of the church, the boredom of the church, I say, "True. And if Jesus Christ would die for a bunch of losers like us, well, there's more than enough hope for you too!"[8] Join us in our adventure of loving Jesus more dearly and following him more nearly. Heaven is a great choir and the rehearsal begins now.

Christians have a decided prejudice toward the communal and the social and against the individual and the solitary. Heaven is a great, holy city, not an exclusive, lonely suburb. Heaven is not only when it's all worship but also when all shall worship. Private prayer for Christians never has quite the traction of public worship. No solo can match an anthem by the whole choir, and no anthem is as good as a hymn sung by the whole congregation. The best things that happen to us—such as our salvation in Jesus Christ—occur *en masse*. Something about Jesus required calling a group of disciples in order to get his salvific revolution in motion.[9]

I also want to say to the critics and scoffers of the church as means of salvation, "Trust me. It takes so long really to know, to accept, to live with, and to obey Jesus (I've been at it over sixty years and look at my continuing failure), don't you want to get started now?" Those who have not recognized their salvation are our responsibilities. None of us lives to ourselves, and none of us dies to ourselves (see 2 Cor 5:14). God does not wish "any to perish, but all to come to repentance" (2 Pet 3:9). Questions of when we shall be saved, whom shall be saved, and how we are being saved are never as interesting as *who* saves.

Paul says that we are, in our sin, "dead."

> But God, who is rich in mercy, out of the great love with which he loved us even when we were dead through our trespasses, made us alive together with Christ—by grace you have been saved—and raised us up with him and seated us with him in the heavenly places in Christ Jesus,

so that in the ages to come he might show the immeasurable riches of his grace in kindness toward us in Christ Jesus. (Eph 2:4-7)

Note that Paul speaks of salvation, our seating "in the heavenly places in Christ Jesus" as now. Salvation begins before we begin and continues long after we thought we were done. Our true place is disclosed as that place where God is. Christ has prepared a place for us: "For it is clear that he [Jesus] did not come to help angels, but the descendants of Abraham" (Heb 2:16), like Zacchaeus.

Furthermore, salvation is more than personal; it is cosmic. The mechanisms of this world, the domination systems, the "rulers . . . authorities . . . cosmic powers . . . spiritual forces of evil in the heavenly places" are considerably more than our "enemies of blood and flesh" (Eph 6:12). Salvation that is merely personal, some new self-understanding that leaves the sun, death, the planets, and every living thing untouched, is hardly worth singing about. Salvation, as depicted in the book of Revelation, is a glorious cosmic victory chant that shouts the completion of God's intentions in creation, "Salvation belongs to our God . . . and to the Lamb!" (Rev 7:10).

Salvation is by God, from sin and death, for a life lived with God, now:

So if anyone is in Christ, there is a new creation: everything old has passed away; see, everything has become new! All this is from God, who reconciled us to himself through Christ, and has given us the ministry of reconciliation; that is, in Christ God was reconciling the world to himself, not counting their trespasses against them, and entrusting the message of reconciliation to us. So we are ambassadors for Christ, since God is making his appeal through us; we entreat you on behalf of Christ, be reconciled to God. (2 Cor 5:17-20)

What Christians name as conversion is not a decision that we make regarding a set of beliefs or a status that we have as validated by a subjective experience. Conversion is waking up to the discovery that we are now living in a different place than we had supposed. Our primary citizenship has been changed. There is a new creation.

In the sixth grade this blond kid shows up one day, and our teacher informs us that the new member of the class is from Poland. He is a "displaced person" who has come to live in Greenville after the war.

"Things are bad in Poland," our teacher tells us.

One classmate punches me in the side and says, "Poland must be hell for somebody to want to move from there to a place that sucks like Greenville."

The kid seemed nice enough, except for his lack of English. But we quickly discovered that the displaced person had a problem: he stole food from people's lunch sacks. Almost everybody had seen him do it. An apple here, a sandwich there. The teacher scolded him. Although he had lunch of his own every day, during the morning recess, he continued to steal food.

One day after a young girl tearfully reported two missing cookies, the teacher called the displaced person up before the class and said, "Look at me! This is America! There's enough food here for everyone. If you ever need food, all you have to do is tell me. The war is over. This isn't Poland!"

And you could see his eyes lighten as if someone was finally making sense. It was the last time he stole. He had awakened to the facts. He had been moved to a different location, exchanged citizenship, no longer displaced—he was home.

Walter Brueggemann characterizes evangelism as "an invitation and summons to 'switch stories,' and therefore to change our lives" [10] Evangelism is also an invitation to receive the strange God in Jesus Christ who has received us strangers—"He has gone to be the guest of a man who is a sinner!"

Israel is that peculiar people formed out of nothing whose vocation it is to serve God and all the peoples, elected to show forth to the world that God, not nations, rules the world. Israel demonstrates what it looks like to be a missionary people who are called to trust God and to be led by God as "the people of God." True, there is always present the temptation to turn this election (and the salvation it makes possible) into exclusion, nationalism, ethnocentrism, and self-trust. Then God's miracle of making "a people out of no people" is sadly perverted. The story of Zacchaeus is a reminder of how difficult it is to love a God who loves so expansively.

The Old Testament spoke of all the nations coming *to* Mount Zion in Jerusalem (Isa 2:2-3; 56:6-7; Zech 14:16-17) in order to be saved. Paul reverses that movement in prophesying a Deliverer, or Christ, coming *out* of Zion into scattered Israel in all the world (Rom 11:26-27).

Church is where we go to be made unhappy with present arrangements. This world is not destined for incineration by God, but rather for fulfillment, completion, healing, and restoration by God. This means that the present world, for all of its occasional beauty, is not God's final act. An early Christian apologist calls Christians "sojourners" who treat their native lands as the "lands of strangers," because followers of Jesus "pass their days on earth, but they are citizens of heaven." [11]

"Are you settling in?" was one of the most frequently asked questions of me during my first couple of years in my present job. Are you settling in?

That is, are you adapting to the status quo? Are you adjusting to what there is without wondering about what shall be? Christians are people who, because we know something about the end, the final purposes of God (that is, heaven) do not settle in. We cultivate sanctified restiveness. We keep moving, keep standing on tiptoes, expectant, because we have been offered a Sunday morning glimpse of a new heaven and a new earth where God at last gets what God wants. Anybody who can say "this is as good as it gets" is either someone who has a very low expectation for what God can do (Deism) or someone who has a very limited circle of friends. Church is thus the antidote to this worldly contentment.

I read in the newspaper about a woman who had raised twelve children, eleven of whom were foster children she had adopted, all of them children with special needs. The newspaper reporter asked her how she, in her limited circumstances, dared to attempt such a thing. What led her to adopt all of these children? She responded, "I saw a new world a'comin'."

Paradoxically, God expands the kingdom of God first through a kind of contraction. As one journeys through Scripture, it is as if there is a gradual narrowing of focus. The story that begins with the creation of the whole lush garden of a world, a few chapters later narrows upon the day-to-day plight of a dusty Near Eastern nomadic family. Yet we find that narrowing to the fortunes of this single family is not the point of the story. The point of the story is vast expansion. The family is given a promise and an assignment. They are elected to witness to the universality of God's reign as the place, the time, and the people through whom God chooses to unfold God's purpose in the world. In the process, Israel is not cast off in favor of some more general, less particular, wider universality but called to show forth the particular, peculiar salvation to all.

As usual, God starts small and specific; this is not a God of myth and abstraction, a God who is anytime and anyplace. So the process of salvation begins in a specific place, an out-of-the-way corner of the world so that salvation might spread like yeast to leaven the whole lump, like light to enlighten the entire world. "He too is a child of Abraham" (Luke 19:9)! The word will spread, not through the world's usual means of violence, coercion, and conquest, but rather through demonstration, through the public witness of a people who point to the truth about what is going on in the world, a people who love to retell and to embody stories, like the one about the day Jesus came to Jericho. It is then that the world has the opportunity to be fascinated by what it sees in Israel and the church, may see that what God has in mind is more than the freeing of a little band of slaves, though that is miraculous enough, but rather has in mind a vast dismantling of empire, a great cosmic homecoming, and release for all people. "He has gone to be the guest of . . . a sinner" (Luke 19:7)! The opened gates through which all enter the heavenly city of John have written upon them the names of the twelve tribes of Israel (Rev 21:10-14).

SALVATION AS ASSIGNMENT

The church participates in rather than supplants Israel's particular vocation to show salvation to all the world. Peculiar Israel is the church's model of both fidelity to the God who saves and the struggle to be a people who are being saved. Salvation is the great treasure that the church—engrafted into the story of Israel—bears in our limited, constricted earthen vessels. So salvation is also an invitation to join up, to be part of a different people, to accept an assignment. Language of decision ("Make a decision for Christ") can never do justice to the peculiar nature of salvation in Christ that, as we have said, is not primarily about any of our choices or decisions but rather about the decisions of God in Christ who chose us before we could choose him. God's gracious Election rather than our decision is the key.

Therefore, to answer the question, "Will this person who is not a member of the church, not in any sense an orthodox believer, be saved?" we must distinguish two aspects contained in the question. If the questioner means, "Is this person a Christian?" the answer is "no." Obviously, this person has not yet heard the gospel in such a way that he has said both "yes" and "I want to be baptized and to become a disciple of Jesus."

But if the question is an inquiry into this person's eternal fate, then as we have said repeatedly, that question is in God's hands completely, in God's own way, and in God's own good time. If this person has yet to feel any sense of God's election and call to discipleship, that's more the church's great challenge than this person's great fault. What effect the failure to hear, to believe, and to follow has on that person's eternal destiny, well, as we have said, that's God's business. Is Zacchaeus now a full-fledged disciple of Jesus? I don't know. That matter is left ambiguous in the story. He has seen something, received something, and responded in a specific way, but who knows? I do know, from my own ineptitude at discipleship that full-fledged disciples are rare.

I know that Paul wrote, "if you confess with your lips that Jesus is Lord and believe in your heart that God raised him from the dead, you will be saved" (Rom10:9), words meant to reassure anxious believers (I suppose) rather than make a sweeping judgment about nonbelievers.[12]

The church is composed of those who confess with our lips and our lives that we have somehow heard our names called by Jesus when he said, "Follow me." I confess that I have often wished the story of my salvation were more dramatic, more interesting. Nothing would please me more than to tell you that I led a life of degeneracy filled with murder and mayhem then I found Jesus and got my life put right. Unfortunately, my salvation is just not that interesting. I got put here by my family when I was an infant, before I could resist. True, I wandered a bit as a youth, but nothing too noteworthy. Eventually I found that my efforts at resistance were futile. I relented; I believed. The folks at the church just wouldn't let me go my own way, took time for me, put up with me; salvation is always a corporate gift rather than a personal attainment. Looking back, I can't believe that church people believed in God enough to believe in me.

My moderate, middle-of-the-road journey toward Jesus seems hardly worth Jesus' dying to save a modestly sinful person like me. The virtues and the vices of us Methodists tend not to be too impressive. Then again, I remember that it was the moderate, middle-of-the-road people who seem to have angered Jesus the most and were well-represented among the mob at his crucifixion. So, here I am, for sure not the most exemplary disciple Jesus ever elected, nor the most dramatically reprobate sinner for whom Jesus died; still, like Paul, by God's grace, I am what I am.

I will note in passing that when Karl Barth celebrated the grand mystery of divine election his prime example was Judas! What sort of Savior would choose a person like Judas to be among his first disciples? The sort of Savior who would chose me.

The church is, therefore, more akin to the relationship that Jesus had with his disciples rather than that which he enjoyed and endured with the multitudes. You will note that Jesus is notoriously more demanding of his disciples than the crowds. Salvation is linked to obedience, responsiveness to the divine summons. To believe in salvation is to acknowledge something as true. It is to wake up to what is. Yet to hold such a belief means that one's life is summoned to be different. Christian belief is linked to Christian witness. Christian believing is not just to adopt some intellectual proposition but rather to get in step with reality, to join up, to have your life subsumed by the one who, despite all the perfectly rational reservations based upon your inadequacies, called you to follow him, to go public with your profession.

One of my churches feeds over a hundred homeless people every morning in Birmingham. The other day, on my way to breakfast with them, I stuck my head in the church's kitchen and recognized a man whom I had met a few weeks before. I was surprised to see him, for I knew that he was a member of one of our most affluent suburban congregations. There he was, washing dishes for homeless people.

I spoke to him and said, "Glad to see you here. Have you always enjoyed working with homeless people?"

"Who told you I enjoyed working with homeless people?" he asked. "Have you met any of those people? A lot of them are crazy, and that's why they're homeless."

Taken aback by his reply, I persisted, "But then how did you get here, washing dishes at seven in the morning for a bunch of homeless people?"

He looked up from his dishwater and said, "I got put here by Jesus, that's how. How did *you* get where you are?" Ah, the mysterious machinations of this salvation of God!

I hold to the statement that we made in *Resident Aliens*. "The only way for the world to know that it is being redeemed is for the church to point to the Redeemer by being a redeemed people."[13] The only way for the world to know that it is the world—namely fallen, corrupt, yet being saved and redeemed—is through the presence of a being saved and being redeemed community, the church. Salvation must have institutional embodiment, for it is hard to keep so strange a story going, over time, across the generations when the triumvirate of the government, the economy, and Hollywood have such powerful means of marginalizing such a story. It's hard to envision new heaven and a new earth, all things restored in Christ, if we do not at least have a glimpse of that future here and now. Left to our own devices, we tend to regard this world with its present princes, powers, and social arrangements as normal. The church's existence is in itself a corporate, material, political claim about salvation that the world cannot smother, despite its best efforts.

[God] has chosen you, because our message of the gospel came to you not in word only, but also in power and in the Holy Spirit and with full conviction . . . so that you became an example to all the believers in Macedonia and in Achaia. For the word of the Lord has sounded forth from you...in every place your faith in God has become known . . . how you turned to God from idols, to serve a living and true God. (1 Thess 1:4-9)

It's therefore our joyful, ecclesiastical election and vocation to be "an ex-ample" to tell the world its true situation now that Jesus Christ has planted his banner in enemy territory and announced that he is willing to do what-ever is necessary to get back what belongs to God.

Modern practices of evangelism tend to put too much stress on the shoulders of the converts for their salvation. Conversion becomes a mat-ter of the will, of belief, or decision by the converts themselves, a product of their wise choices. The driving force behind this characterization of conversion is less Scripture than the shopping mall, the supermarket in which our lives are the products of our astute choices, the sum of our pref-erences. Jesus told his followers to "Go . . . make disciples of all nations" (Matt 28:19), making evangelism a task that God has given to the church, not to the world.

Karl Barth raised the ire of American evangelicals when, after hearing Billy Graham preach, pronounced him "dreadful" because he disapproved of what he took to be Dr. Graham's attempt to drive people toward salva-tion by hammering them for their sins. Barth said that you preach salva-tion first, joyfully announcing an event by which God has decisively acted in our behalf. Only in the light of that accomplished fact is one able to speak of sin. One knows the seriousness of sin only in the light of the cross. The cross unmasks our sin while removing it. First is the joyful an-nouncement of salvation, salvation accomplished in Christ, then the mod-est, grateful human "yes."

To be "saved" is to know that our lives are dependent upon God to preserve us and to remember us. We cannot sustain ourselves by ourselves. Most of the violence that we commit arises from our godless attempts to secure our lives on our terms rather than God's. Sadly, there is more than a touch of the coercive and at least the incipiently violent in some of our so-called evangelism as we construct our knock-down arguments for sal-vation in Jesus, making Jesus virtually irresistible in a way that is unfaith-ful to Jesus. The evangelical penchant for speaking of evangelism as a rescue contest with its talk of *winning* and *reaching* doesn't quite fit the no-tion of salvation that we've developed here as including, inviting, recog-nizing, adopting, joining, and announcing.

When we proclaim salvation we are calling people to whom they are created to be in fellowship with God. In salvation humanity's failure—our alienation from God and from our sisters and brothers—is overcome by God. People hear the message of salvation and receive it because of the work of the Holy Spirit (Gal 3:2-5; Rom 10:17). Because salvation is received by us as a gift that is offered, a miraculous work of a living God, humanly considered, salvation has a certain "passive" quality. And although I do not mean to defend the boredom of the church, I realize that sometimes salvation as enacted within the church may seem to the world to be less than spectacular. The church's claim is that salvation is not supposed to be spectacular. This is God's normality, the ordinary state of things once God gets what God wants.

In salvation, we are given freedom from our desperate efforts to justify our own lives—to secure ourselves by our accumulation of stuff or by our achievements, material and spiritual—because down deep we fear that we are not valued, not sought, and not loved by the One in whom we live and move and have our being. In salvation we discover that our lives are valuable not because of what we achieve, but rather in what we are given by the God who seeks us in Christ.

Though I in no way would want to let us off the hook for our evangelistic failures—the church is less interesting than Jesus—I do think it important to admit that some of our "failures" to reach people in the name of Christ *are due to Jesus*. Salvation is being with Jesus, here, now. We followers of Jesus ought to, of all people, know how difficult that can be. To be brought into his reach is rescue, reward, and redemption for some people but it is also pain, relinquishment, and sacrifice for others. Salvation for all is not only deliverance from affliction of evil and death but also Jesus' command never to inflict evil or death on anyone else. As Amos said, salvation tends to be both deliverance and judgment at the same time (Amos 5:18-20).

When I once lamented the small proportion of students who attended our services at the university chapel, a student comforted me, "Go easy on yourself. Your message is against just about everything we're giving our lives to around here. Students have enough sense to know that following Jesus could only make our lives more difficult. I'm amazed that you have so many who show up!"

Smart young man, that one.

The love that moves the sun and the stars now moves us. "For the love of Christ urges us on, because we are convinced that one has died for all; therefore all have died" (2 Cor 5:14). Conviction that Christ has died for all motivates us to deal with all in a different way, urged on by the love of Christ. We nobodies, now embraced by Christ as somebodies are unable to consider anybody a nobody. Jesus had a gift for noticing people who were beyond our notice—the poor widow who put the tiny coin in the offering, the single lost sheep, the one lost coin. To be noticed by Jesus is to be saved, to notice yourself as if for the first time, and to be worthy of note by all those whom Jesus has noted.

Surely this is what Paul means when he says "from now on . . . we regard no one from a human point of view" (2 Cor 5:16). Everyone is reviewed as someone for whom Christ died for their salvation. We are forced to conform our views of other people to how God sees people.[14] We are enjoined, by this God, not to seek justice—which in its own way would be progress enough—but rather to love, actively to seek risky, self-involving relationship, to love as God has loved us. Zacchaeus learned how costly it is to be loved by Christ, not only in the disbursement of his goods in restitution, but also in the anger and disapproval of his neighbors. Such is the destiny, sometimes, of those who are saved by Christ.

In one of my predominantly African American churches, a pastor was leading a discussion in which the subject of heaven arose. A layperson, whose family had suffered in Birmingham during the civil rights movement, said, "If there's a chance that Bull Connor might be in heaven, then I don't want to be there."

"Oh," pled the pastor, "please don't say that. Bull and I just can't be happy there without you too!" Bull Connor was a Methodist.

Stanley Hauerwas defines salvation as "being engrafted into practices that save us from those powers that would rule our lives making it impossible for us to truly worship God."[15] True, as long as we stress that the "practices that save us" are also aspects of the salvific work of God. It takes more than good habits, even truthful ones, to save such sinners. I worry that the current characterization of Christianity as a set of "practices" could be just another means of rendering the Christian faith into something that we do rather than a way of being shocked by what God in Christ has done and is doing. Even though it is wonderful that Zacchaeus initiated noteworthy practices of almsgiving and restitution, all of this is but response to the miracle that, "Today salvation has come to this house . . . because [this one] too is a son of Abraham" (Luke 19:9).

Every congregation, every church becomes a sort of test of the truth of "this salvation of God." The light on a lampstand gives light to "all in the house" (Matt 5:15). It would have been so much easier for us if Jesus had merely said that he was the light for his faithful followers, not for the whole world, not for all. And it would have been easier if Jesus had said that he was the light of the world. Alas, for the vocation of the church, Jesus said that we were! It would have been safer for us if only Jesus had gone to a cross rather than promising that there is a cross to fit our backs too. Walk into a church on Sunday morning and search carefully to see if you can get a glimpse of the kingdom of God taking bodily form. Does this gathering look, to some marked degree, like salvation as it has met us in Jesus? Do you get a sense of the extravagantly wide embrace, the reach, the risk, the universality of Christ's love? Do you fear that there will be grumbling all around town because of the sort of riffraff, high and low, that Jesus hangs with? In my experience, a congregation that's too small in its thinking, introverted, limited to the spiritual needs of one generation, unilingual rather than multilingual, is a group of people trying to be church with a too constrained soteriology. Over half of the churches in my conference have not made one new disciple of Jesus in the past two years. In the majority of the churches I serve, a too timid soteriology is literally killing us.

Jesus told a parable about two men who went to the temple to pray (Luke 18:10-14). One prayed, in effect, "God I thank thee that I am saved, not like these sinners who are lost."

The other man prayed, in effect, "God have mercy on me the lost!"

Do you remember which one Jesus said went down to his house "justified," that is made right with God, atoned, found? Oh the risk, on any Sunday morning, of daring to be in conversation with a God who saves! The risk of believing that "Jesus saves" is that the one who told the parable about the two men at the temple saves.

One implication of salvation in Christ for me as a pastor, which I find more annoying than invigorating, is that because Jesus saves, then no situation in my church is hopeless. No affliction and no infliction of evil is possible finally to prevail. Human beings are salvageable. I know that drug addiction is a horrible, virtually irreversible curse. I know that spouse abuse is almost never "curable." Still, I know a host of gospel stories that assert—all social science to the contrary—that we are ultimately redeemable.

I know that a great number of Americans are opposed to unlimited immigration across our borders. Still, I worship a Savior who saves, reaches, and invites without regard to national borders. "When are we going to do something about undocumented workers?" someone asked me recently. I thought to myself, "Give Jesus time; he will."

Another pastoral implication is that human beings are not the source of our own salvation—or anybody else's. It's tough enough for me to know that I can't save myself. But it's also hard to believe (and perhaps this is a problem only for us pastors) that I am not the source of someone else's salvation. I can tell the story, I can trot out my little arguments, I can sit with them and try to be a good example for them, I can go out into the night and seek them, but I am not the Christ. I'm only an ambassador. I witness under the conviction that Christ wants this life, that Christ is already active in this life before I got there, and that Christ will continue to work in this life long after I've gone on to whatever Jesus has in store for me next. But only Jesus saves.

Sometimes we pastors try to be the messiahs for our people rather than to let the Messiah save them. In such moments we imply that their salvation is through a competent, capable pastor who enables them to get their act together. No. Salvation is allowing Jesus to intrude among us, as he is, rather than as we would have him to be. In my experience, any pastor who is overworked to the point of disillusionment and exhaustion is probably due for a refurbished soteriology.

And one more evangelical, soteriological implication: church growth is not a program of Fuller Seminary, not just an attempt to pump up a flagging institutional church. Growth is a mark of the church. "All" is quantity rather than quality. Any congregation that is not growing—not restlessly probing the world, not reaching with Christ, not curious about what new beachhead Christ has obtained lately, not getting hammered by the world for having lunch with people like Zacchaeus—is not a fully faithful church. Just me and my friends, the cognoscenti, huddled about the blessed Eucharist, or enjoying God's pure word, or following Christian practices, or caressing our correct Reformed doctrine, or reveling in our warm Wesleyan heritage, or affirming the right social attitudes and the truly righteous political stance—without growth—is not the church of the seeking shepherd, the searching woman, or the one who was crucified for eating and drinking with too many sinners.

"So, it's all about numbers, is it?" This is the predictable response to my connection of ecclesiology and growth. It is unimaginable that Saint Luke, Saint Paul, or Saint John Wesley would understand the alibis that are offered for church decline and death under the guise that we are so faithful to Jesus, so theologically responsible that we are dying by attrition. Is it all about numbers? Take it up with Jesus. Explain why so many of his parables of the kingdom of God are parables of growth—the yeast that leavens the whole lump, the tiny seed that produces miraculous harvest, the three talents that are invested to make three talents more, the handful of disciples that eventually become a great wave that swept over the whole world. Can you say "all"?

When asked why the Episcopal Church in America is in precipitous decline, the presiding bishop replied that most of the growth in growing churches is through births to parents who are already church members and that the Episcopal Church, since it draws upon the better educated classes of society has a lower birthrate so therefore. . . . Not one of the presiding bishop's better thoughts, I think.

Alas, too many of us church leaders have been content to hunker down in the vineyard (Matthew 20) with the few faithful who have been bequeathed to us by the evangelism of previous generations rather than join the master of the vineyard in his forays to the unemployment office. John Wesley knew enough about the expansive quality of salvation in Jesus' name to ask of prospective preachers, not only about their vocation, their gifts and graces, but also about their fruit. When we settle down and become parochial, the Holy Spirit drifts elsewhere, Jesus leaves us as his movement keeps on the move. There is something about Jesus that refuses to bed down with the sheep who are either too unimaginative or too decrepit to wander. I just closed a church after a seventy-year run. Their dying words were, "There is no one anywhere near our church who might join our church." What they meant is, "We are in the middle of great population growth that is all of a color and a language other than our own and it makes us uncomfortable that Jesus expects us to recognize them as part of us." Church growth is an expected, essential byproduct of a Savior who is relentlessly out on the prowl for fresh disciples. Church decline is an expected result for a church that refuses to follow a Savior who is relentlessly out to grow God's kingdom.

It really gets me that Kentucky Fried Chicken loves the people of West Birmingham more than my church loves them, has found a way to build and maintain the best-looking place in West Birmingham whereas we United Methodists have mostly abandoned that part of the city. Belief in Christian salvation should produce a church at least as compassionate and bold as a business that sells soggy chicken.

I am therefore determined that our church will establish a congregation in a prison in Alabama. John Wesley thought that there wasn't much wrong with any Christian that couldn't be cured by joining God's work in prisons. I am told that the engine of Black Muslim growth in North America is proselytism in prisons. I am unaware if Muhammad ever was jailed or had good friends doing time. I know that Jesus did both. Our Savior was a prisoner on death row and just about all of our heroes—Peter and Paul for instance—witnessed from a jail cell. About half of the New Testament, by my estimate, was written in jail. We should be ashamed that we have so neglected this obviously God-given opportunity for church growth that is offered us by the most imprisoned country in the world.

Distinctive discipleship and ecclesiology does not exclude missional reach and inclusion; it is the major rationale for mission and evangelism. When asked by a reporter to define my church's policy on illegal immigration I responded that we would rely on our politicians to work out the details of just immigration policy but that some of the most spectacular United Methodist growth in the United States was due to newly established Spanish-speaking congregations. For some reason Methodism—that bores most ethnic groups, judging from the numbers—thrills people who speak Spanish. Therefore, we Methodists were opposed to any wall, policy, or government practice that hinders the Hispanic surge into our churches! God has found a great way to ignite us United Methodists and nothing should be done to dampen Hispanic enthusiasm for helping our church be reborn. "Mr. Bush, tear down this wall!"

Such are the politics of those who believe that the one and only way, truth, and life is a Savior named Jesus, little Jesus, the one God who was built low to the ground, the Savior who stooped.

AT THE END, GOD

This sermon on salvation is nearing its conclusion. But salvation is a subject that resists neat finales. There's a reason so many of Jesus' parables don't have endings. The story continues. "The World is not Conclusion," wrote Emily Dickinson, "A Species stands beyond / Invisible. . . . It beckons, and it baffles."[16] The disastrous turn of the modern world was when it concluded that here is all there is. The world is not a conclusion, not only in the sense that there might be more world in some hereafter but that there is more going on right now than our thought can do justice to. It's not over until God says it's over. Reality is not limited by our powers of perception; reality is whatever depth God creates it to be. Behind our busyness or lack of it, God is busy. That which arises out of us is not the conclusion of all that is operative upon us. Be warned: God's story continues.

Reading a book about salvation is not salvation. Reading a book may be an incitement to faith, but never a conclusion. God didn't just give us a book, the Bible; we got Jesus the Christ, a person who makes a move on us. Our wisdom begins where it ends in him, desire for him being better than information about him. A book, I believe, can be used by the Holy

Spirit to introduce someone to salvation, but it does not constitute it. So it is now time to throw aside this book and get on with the joy of becoming accustomed to Jesus and the ones whom he so costly loves. Therein is our, and the world's, salvation.

"We shall never forget their sacrifice," said a speaker at this past year's Memorial Day celebration. Though he meant well, his statement was a lie; only about fifty people gathered to remember the sacrifice of the fallen soldiers, even though everyone in town had the day off. Our powers of recollection are no match for the sting of death.

The psalmist pleads, "Do not remember the sins of my youth . . . remember me" (Ps 25:7). Whereas the sins of my youth are nothing to brag about, it is important that in the end God remembers me. Our hope is that God has a good recall for names.

One day I shall leave home and shall not return that evening. I shall then be buried, forgotten, returned to the dust from whence I was made, remembered for a while only by those few who knew me well. I shall fade into the oblivion of the forgotten. All my books, including this one, shall be cast on the great remainder table of history, shall crumble to dust and be forgotten. Whatever I accomplished shall tarnish and diminish.

And yet, on the basis of what I have known of God, I believe that what seemed a conclusion will in reality be a commencement. I fully expect to hear the God who so sought me in life stoop down to me in death, saying, "Yes, the face is familiar. I remember you. And where are the others you were to bring with you? Oh well, I've got a whole new world to show you, a large family, a great city. I never gave up on you. Can we talk? You haven't seen anything yet. We've got all the time in the world."

This is our salvation.

A CONCLUDING
POSTSCRIPT

Being from South Carolina and in church for so long that I forgot what it was like not to be there, I had few doubts that God had me—I might as well relax and enjoy it. I became interested in your salvation through Karl Barth (particularly Volume IV of his Church Dogmatics*), to whom I have referred throughout this meditation. A sustained reading of* Church Dogmatics IV, *while I was a student at Yale Divinity School, remains the most important theological event of my ministry. As an Arminian, that is, a Wesleyan, I knew that Jesus Christ died for all and not just a few. Yet Barth taught me how that affirmation—all— was at the heart of the life, death, and resurrection of Jesus Christ. As a seminarian, thinking about letting God take my life for Christian ministry, I was moved by Barth's doctrine of reconciliation. Christ gave his life for humanity, particularly the backward, wayward among them, so I could too. The best moves in my ministry—like being called to be a bishop in Alabama—were derivative of my theological conviction that Jesus Christ really does reach to sinners. All.*

In nearly forty years of ministry, I've had occasion to ask Christ why he died not just for me and my close friends but for all. I never get so experienced in faith, adept in the grace of God as to be incapable of shock that "at the right time Christ died for the ungodly" (Rom 5:6). An unfailingly renewable resource for the work of ministry is the continuing astonishment that Christ died for the very ones whom I find to be such a pain in the neck. If I'm going to worship Christ, I've got to go to his table with the ones for whom he died. I've got to be where he is. Once when asked why so few people joined her work with the poor, Mother Teresa replied that in the poor we meet Jesus in his most disturbing, demanding guise—no wonder we avoid the poor.

More recently I've been helped by Richard John Neuhaus's essays in The Eternal Pity *also his* Death on a Friday Afternoon.[1] *Upon moving to Alabama, I reread the stories of Flannery O'Connor, which reminded me that only a God who is willing to suffer the most violent of deaths for the most stupid of people would do any of us any good.[2] A few years ago I was introduced to the deep and demanding Hans Urs von Balthasar.[3] These three Catholics told me what needed to be said. I should also credit my rereading of Kierkegaard, whose insights on the oddity of*

135

Christian faith and the absurdity of Christian salvation crop up throughout the pages of this book.

Sunday morning in a dreary little church in the Midlands of England, a stereotypical English pensioner—sensible shoes, hair in a bun—arose to read the appointed Epistle, Hebrews 12:18-29:

> You have not come to something that can be touched, a blazing fire, and dark-ness, and gloom, and a tempest, and the sound of a trumpet, and a voice whose words made the hearers beg not another word be spoken to them. . . . But you have come to Mount Zion and to the city of the living God, the heavenly Jerusalem, and to innumerable angels in festal gathering. (vv. 18-19, 22)

I had to restrain my impulse to laugh aloud at this little lady, clipped British monotone speech barely audible, reading about "blazing fire" and "tempest." Those words in this setting, read by her, were comical, absurd even.

Well, this is the church—a group of well-meaning, but insignificant, rather forlorn older folks gathered before a story with words that are too great, too grand for us to handle.

Then we stood as the priest (a sweet little man adorned in a beatific grin) in-effectually read the Gospel for the day, Luke 13:10-17, the story of Jesus heal-ing the crooked woman: The faithful gather for a restful Sabbath service. All is serene—until Jesus shows up. Jesus reaches out, touches and heals the afflicted woman who has suffered for so long. The devoted are outraged at his desecration of the Sabbath. Jesus notices, embraces, frees, saves a suffering person on the margins—and the gathered faithful despise him for it. This is the church.

And yet where else is this true story told? Who but the poor old, comical church has the wisdom and the guts to tell such a tale? The story is the hope of the world and the judgment of the church at the same time. Where will the world hear the truth about God if not from those who are elected to tell the story? There are only us to tell the tale. This "salvation of God" is also the church. Thanks be to God.

NOTES

Preface

1. *Good News* (November–December 2006), 42.
2. Ibid.

1. The God Who Refuses to Be Alone

1. W. H. Auden, "The More Loving One," W. H. *Auden: Selected Poems*, ed. Edward Mendelson (London: Faber and Faber, 1979), 237.
2. One "exchristian" (at the website *exchristian.com*) even complains that it is diversity of images and ideas for Christian salvation that led him to give up on the Christian faith: "One would think a perfect God who knows 'everything'. . . would have directed His followers to write *one* sacred book [that would] detail just exactly how one is to be 'saved' and that this plan would be uniformly followed. . . . One would think that Christianity would agree on just exactly how one is 'saved.'. . . Once again, confusion reigns!" What this critic calls confusion and bewildering complexity we celebrate as a richness that defies single definition. The allegedly tolerant folk at *religioustolerance.org*, after surveying the New Testament on "salvation" complain that it's impossibly "ambiguous" and "chaotic," which suggests to me a sad intolerance for biblical richness. For a comprehensive study of biblical texts on the theme of salvation, see Joel B. Green, *Salvation* (St. Louis: Chalice Press, 2003). Green says that salvation, "is the comprehensive term for all the benefits that are graciously bestowed on humans by God" (9).
3. *International Herald Tribune* (Paris, February 21, 1990).
4. Karl Barth, *Church Dogmatics*, IV, 1 (Edinburgh, Scotland: T&T Clark, 1961), 8.
5. Karl Barth, *Table Talk*, ed. J. D. Godsey (London: Oliver and Boyd, 1963), 62.
6. Karl Barth, *Dogmatics in Outline* (New York: Harper and Bros., 1959), 109.
7. Ibid., 170.
8. My allegorical interpretation of the story is that of Charles Wesley in his poem on the good Samaritan from the point of view of the victim. Augustine also interprets the parable as a christological allegory (which C. H. Dodd, in his great book on the parables, ridicules, as I recall).
9. Karl Barth, *Church Dogmatics*, II, 2 (Edinburgh, Scotland: T&T Clark, 1957), 14.

10. Miscellanies, 104 as cited by David Willis, *Clues to the Nicene Creed* (Grand Rapids, Mich.: Eerdmans, 2005), 49.

11. *Institutes*, 3, 10, 2, McNeill, ed., 720–21.

2. The Eros of God

1. Dietrich Bonhoeffer, *Letters and Papers from Prison*, ed. Eberhard Bethge (New York: Macmillan, 1972), 303.

2. Sura 4:157

3. C. S. Lewis, *Surprised by Joy* (New York: Harcourt, Brace, and World, 1955), 229.

4. X. J. Kennedy, "In a Prominent Bar in Secaucus One Day," *Nude Descending a Staircase* (New York: Doubleday, 1961).

5. In his *The Divine Names*, Pseudo-Dionysius comments that whereas *eros* is not found in the New Testament, *zelos* ("zeal") is and that zeal means the same thing as *eros*. He notes that one of the great challenges of the Christian life is worshiping a zealot of a God!

6. Charles Wesley, "Love Divine, All Loves Excelling." *The United Methodist Hymnal* (Nashville: The United Methodist Publishing House, 1989), number 384.

3. Divine Abundance

1. Sigmund Freud, *New Introductory Lectures in Psychoanalysis*, trans. James Strachey (New York, W. W. Norton and Co., 1965), 147.

2. Karl Barth, *Deliverance to the Captives*, trans. Marguerite Wieser (New York: Harper & Row, 1961), 85–92.

3. Richard Dawkins, *The God Delusion* (Boston: Houghton Mifflin Co., 2006).

4. With C. C. Carlson (Grand Rapids, Mich.: Zondervan, 1972).

5. What follows is heavily indebted to the arguments and illustrations given by Richard John Neuhaus in his *Death on a Friday Afternoon: Meditations on the Last Words of Jesus from the Cross* (New York: Basic Books, 2000) as well as his *The Eternal Pity: Reflections on Dying* (South Bend, Ind.: University of Notre Dame Press, 2000).

6. Karl Barth, *Church Dogmatics*, IV, 4 (Edinburgh, Scotland: T&T Clark, 1969), 21.

7. Karl Barth, *Church Dogmatics*, II, 2 (Edinburgh, Scotland: T&T Clark, 1957), 639.

8. Barth, *Church Dogmatics* IV, 2 (Edinburgh, Scotland: T&T Clark, 1961), 271.

9. Ibid., 518.

10. Karl Barth, *Church Dogmatics*, IV, 3 (Edinburgh, Scotland: T&T Clark, 1961), 477.

11. Ibid.

12. Ibid., 477–78.

13. *Explanatory Notes on the New Testament* (London: Epworth, 1950), Acts 10:35.

14. In his "The Scripture Way of Salvation," John Wesley noted that the tense of the verb *sesomenoi* in Ephesians 2:8, can be translated (as it was in the KJV) as "Ye are saved," admitting that with equal propriety it could be translated "Ye *have been* saved." (The NRSV and NIV use the later translation.) Wesley would have me add that it's important both to affirm salvation as an accomplished fact that is no longer under dispute and an event with continuing world-changing significance.

15. Many Wesleyan hymns, including this one by Charles Wesley, stress this universal redemption and God's desire for all:

Come, sinners, to the gospel feast;
Let every soul be Jesus' guest.
Ye need not one be left behind,
For God hath bid all humankind.
("Come, Sinners, to the Gospel Feast," *The United Methodist Hymnal* [Nashville:
The United Methodist Publishing House, 1989], number 339)

4. Christ Triumphant

1. Encyclical, *Redemptoris Missio* 4, 6, 9, 11.

2. Franz Rosenzweig, *The Star of Redemption*, trans. from the second ed. of 1930 by William W. Hallo (New York: Holt, Rinehart and Winston, 1971), part 3.

3. Geoffrey Wainwright, *Doxology: The Praise of God in Worship, Doctrine and Life: A Systematic Theology* (London: Epworth Press, 1980), note 1134.

4. Creed found in the Presbyterian Church U.S.A., *Book of Confessions*, 29. David Willis, *Clues to the Nicene Creed* (Grand Rapids, Mich.: Eerdmans, 2005), 127.

5. (New York: Hatchette Book Group, 2007).

6. Karl Barth, *Church Dogmatics*, III, 3 (Edinburgh, Scotland: T&T Clark, 1960), 138.

7. Karl Barth, *Church Dogmatics*, IV, 3 (Edinburgh, Scotland: T&T Clark, 1961), 477.

8. "Thy darling attribute I praise. . . . Thy universal love" from "Universal Redemption," *The Works of John Wesley, The Sermons*, ed. Albert C. Outler (Nashville: Abingdon Press, 1984), 3:560.

9. Pseudo-Dionysius, *The Complete Works*, ed. P. Rorem, *Classics of Western Spirituality* (New York: Paulist Press, 1987), 75.

5. Damned?

1. C. S. Lewis, *Mere Christianity* (New York: Macmillan, 1944), 115.

2. Interview on WUNC, November 13, 2006.

3. Augustine's *Enchiridion* 8, in Augustine, *The Enchiridion on Faith, Hope, and Love*, ed. Henry Paolucci (Chicago: Regnery Gateway, 1961).

4. Whereas Arminianism tends to stress the importance of human freedom to choose, I fear that, in the modern context, Arminianism has been corrupted by contemporary notions of unfettered individual autonomy to the point that we have given *freedom* a bad name.

5. H. Richard Niebuhr, *The Kingdom of God in America* (New York: Harper Torchbooks, 1937), 193. Recent research by the Barna Group reveals that the main reason that young adult non-Christians give for their negative assessment of the Christian faith (87 percent) is that "present-day Christianity is judgmental" (www.barna.org, accessed September 24, 2007).

6. In his critique of Origen in his *City of God*, XXI, 17, Augustine says Origen's views on salvation are too "compassionate." That strikes me as a curious critique of any viewpoint that presumes to be Christian.

7. See "Hellfire and Damnation: Four Ancient and Modern Views" in George Hunsinger, *Disruptive Grace: Studies in the Theology of Karl Barth* (Grand Rapids, Mich.: Eerdmans, 2000), 226–52.

8. Karl Barth, *Church Dogmatics*, IV, 1 (Edinburgh, Scotland: T&T Clark, 1961), 309.

9. Emil Brunner, *The Christian Doctrine of Creation and Redemption* (Philadelphia: Westminster Press, 1949), 118.

10. N. T. Wright, in *Surprised by Hope: Rethinking Heaven, the Resurrection, and the Mission of the Church* (New York: HarperCollins, 2008), doesn't think that purgatory is worth defending or reconstructing—unbiblical, wishful thinking (Wright dismisses contemporary "purgatory-for-all" as so much sentimental universalism). Yet Wright has an intriguing suggestion about purgatory. He says, "*The myth of purgatory is an allegory, a projection from the present on the future*" (148, italics his). Though he means this as a criticism, I take it as an insightful compliment. Based on all we know of the seeking, waiting, searching, and resourceful God in Scripture and in this life, purgatory is a reasonable projection of God's relation to us in whatever life awaits.

11. Quoted by Tom Long, *Testimony: Talking Ourselves into Being Christian* (San Francisco: Jossey-Bass, 2004) 126.

12. Samuel Beckett, *Proust* (New York: Grove Press, 1957), 1.

13. P. T. Forsyth, *This Life and the Next* (Boston: The Pilgrim Press, 1948), 37.

14. *Time* (August 20, 2007), 44.

15. Richard J. Neuhaus, ed., *The Eternal Pity: Reflections on Dying* (South Bend, Ind.: University of Notre Dame Press, 2000), 54–70.

6. What About Them?

1. Karl Barth, *Church Dogmatics*, IV, 3 (Edinburgh, Scotland: T&T Clark, 1961), 342.

2. Marcus Borg, *The Heart of Christianity: Rediscovering a Life of Faith* (San Francisco: HarperSanFrancisco, 2004), 218.

3. John Calvin, *Institutes of the Christian Religion* 3.2.7, McNeill ed. (Philadelphia: Westminster Press, 1960), 551.

4. Quoted in Nicholas Lash, *Believing Three Ways in One God: A Reading of the Apostles' Creed* (South Bend, Ind.: University of Notre Dame Press, 1993), 80.

7. Strange Salvation

1. N. T. Wright, *Jesus and the Victory of God* (Minneapolis: Fortress Press, 1996).

2. James H. Cone, *God of the Oppressed*, rev. ed. (Maryknoll, N.Y.: Orbis, 1997), 42-49.

3. Wright, *Jesus and the Victory of God*.

4. Rick Founds, "Lord, I Lift Your Name on High." Copyright Maranatha Praise, Inc./ASCAP. All rights reserved.

5. Immanuel Kant, *Critique of Pure Reason* A 805/B 833, ed. and trans. P. Guyer and A. Wood (Cambridge: Cambridge University Press, 1999).

6. The phrase is first used by Cyprian, later much modified by Augustine in his *De Baptismo contra Donatistas*, bk. 4, ch. 17, section 24.

7. John Wesley, *A Farther Appeal to Men of Reason and Religion* 1, 3, 1975; 11:106.

8. Speaking of boring, I just watched Tim Russert interview a presidential candidate on *Meet the Press*. This is the exciting TV experience that people are watching at home rather than coming to church?

9. This theological affirmation ("no salvation outside the church") makes all the more bizarre that on any given Sunday fewer than a third of United Methodists are actually at

church. An unbelieving world is fully justified in wondering, "If church is essential for salvation, why do the majority of church members avoid attending church?"

10. Walter Brueggemann, *Biblical Perspectives on Evangelism: Living in a Three-Storied Universe* (Nashville: Abingdon Press, 1993), 11.

11. "The Epistle to Diognetus," in *Ante-Nicene Fathers*, vol. 1, trans. and ed. Alexander Roberts and James Donaldson (Peabody, Mass.: Hendrickson, 1994), 26–27. Compare with Philippians 3:20.

12. A recent study of why North American Muslims convert to Christianity revealed that the most attractive aspect of the Christian faith was to be given certainty of salvation. One Indonesian woman spoke of her fear, based upon a tradition attributed to Muhammad, that the bridge over hell on the way to paradise is as thin as a hair.

13. (Nashville: Abingdon Press, 1989), 94.

14. This is a small thing, but I commend it to you as helpful. I try to spend an hour a week in conversation with someone who is not a Christian. I have found this to be a valuable spiritual discipline, giving me, the consummate insider, a feel for what it is like to be an outsider. A hour a week with a misunderstanding, uncomprehending nonbeliever gives me some small indication of what it must be like for Jesus to spend an hour a week with me.

15. *In Good Company: The Church as Polis* (South Bend, Ind.: University of Notre Dame Press, 1995), 8.

16. Emily Dickinson, "This World is not Conclusion," *The Complete Poems of Emily Dickinson* (New York: Little, Brown & Company, 1960).

A Concluding Postscript

1. Richard J. Neuhaus, ed., *The Eternal Pity: Reflections on Dying* (South Bend, Ind.: University of Notre Dame Press, 2000) and *Death on a Friday Afternoon* (New York: Basic Books, 2000).

2. Flannery O'Connor, *The Collected Works* (New York: Literary Classics of the United States, 1988).

3. Hans Urs von Balthasar, *Theo-Drama*, vol. 4 (San Francisco: Ignatius, 1994) and, more particularly, *Dare We Hope "That All Men Be Saved"?* trans. David Kipp and Lothar Krauth (San Francisco: Ignatius Press, 1988).

SCRIPTURE INDEX

Genesis

1	5, 14, 17
1–2	45, 46
8:21	17

Exodus

14:13	4, 27
14:30	27
15:2	4
23:9	54
32	16
32:10	16

Job

9:20-21	62
9:22	62
12:4-6	62
12:7-25	62
13:3	62
16:7-9	62
21:7	62
38:1	62
42:1-6	62
42:5	62

Psalms

25:7	134
36:6	40
65:5	4
74:12	4
121:1	64
139:7-8	70
145:15-16	64

Song of Solomon

3:1-4	21–22

Isaiah

2:2-3	122
11:9	51
12:2	5
40:10-11	65
45:8	5
49:6	96
54:7	65
55	4
55:8	73
56:6-7	122

Zechariah

14:16-17	122

Matthew

1:21	5
1:23	23
4:17	6
5	38
5:3	7
5:14	40
5:15	31
5:40-42	12
5:45	38
5:48	38
6:10	58
7:13	99
7:23	76
11:28	40

(Matthew—continued)
13:25 80
15:37 40
18:15-22 72
19:26 87
20 . . . . 52, 88, 132
20:1-11 77
20:14-16 88
21:31 98
22:10 40
23:12 40
24:14 40
25 . . . . 71, 75, 77
25:14-30 . . . . 76, 82
25:19 82
25:24-25 82
25:30 83
25:31-46 . . . . 70, 71
25:40 54
25:41-46 76
25:46 70
26:69-75 41
28:19 . . . . 40, 127
28:19-20 60
28:20 59

Mark
1:15 6
1:41 6
8 36–37
9:38-50 108
10:21 12
10:27 47
10:45 108
11:9 5
11:17 40

Luke
1:69 6
1:46-55 23
1:77-78 6
3:6 38
4:16-30 81
5:27-32 112
5:32 112
6:20 6

9:23 . . . . 12, 28
10 10
11:20 6
13:6-9 80
13:7 80
13:8 80
13:10-17 136
13:23 69
13:24 69
13:34 80
13:35 80
14:13-14 53
15 . . . . 7, 36, 79, 110
15:2 . . . . 7, 40, 110
15:31 66
16:8 77
16:9-18 27
16:19-31 72
16:22 72
18:10-14 130
18:18 54
19:1-10 . . . . 109, 112
19:3 109
19:7 . . . . 110, 124
19:9 . . . . 110, 112, 123, 129
19:9-10 110
19:10 11
21:28 64
23:34 86
23:34, 43 55
23:43 . . . . 65, 89
24:13-35 7

John
1 5
1:9 40
1:10 79
1:10-11 101
1:14 5
1:46 106
3 78
3:13 43
3:16 46
4:22 . . . . 6, 25
6 64
8:48 11

9:22 100
9:39 78
10:7, 11 99
10:16 . . . . 47, 101, 102
12:24 12
12:31-32 90
12:32 . . . . 40, 64, 76, 102
12:47-48 . . . . 79, 83
14 . . . . 100, 101
14:1 . . . . 98, 99, 100
14:2 100
14:2-3 99
14:3 99
14:5 . . . . 100, 101
14:6 . . . . 13, 23, 100, 101
14:7 . . . . 99, 101
14:8 101
14:19 79
15:12 13
15:13 12
15:16 . . . . 44, 82
16:33 . . . . 58, 79
17:3 13
19:13 78
20 . . . . 17, 78
21:19 98
21:22 102

Acts
1:8 40
2 41
2:14-47 41
2:29 41
2:40 9
3:21 47
4:10-12 116
4:12 . . . . 32, 42, 93–94
4:13, 29 41
4:30 42
4:32 41
9 118
9:2 98
9:15 97
10:34 97
10:34-35 50
13:47 96

22:4 98
26:26 41
28:28 . . . . 10, 39, 41

Romans
1:4 42
1:16 . . . . 41, 42
1:18 79
3:20 96
3:21 42
4 97
5 18
5:1 42
5:6 . . . . 119, 135
5:6-10 17
5:9 42
5:11 42
5:12-21 . . . . 58, 77
5:15, 17 25
5:18 108
6:23 43
7:24 32
8 115
8:1 42
8:19-22 88
8:22 28
8:38 41
8:39 59
9:17-18 120
10:9 124–25
10:10 41
10:17 127
11:15 41
11:26 42
11:26-27 122
11:32 . . . . 38, 77
11:33-34 108
11:33-36 42
12:19 78
12:29 49
13:1 83
14:7-9 84
14:17 42
15:7 97
15:19 42
16:25 42

1 Corinthians
1:18-21 81
1:22-23 x
1:24 42
1:27 78
2:6-10 41
3:15 71
3:22-23 41
4:4 76
4:7 25
6:2-3 41
13:13 42
15:24 56
15:26 26
15:28 . . . . 47, 87
15:54 63
15:54-57 41

2 Corinthians
1:18-21 59
1:20 79
4:7 42
5:4 63
5:10 . . . . 78, 79
5:14 . . . . 108, 120, 128
5:16 129
5:17-20 121
5:18 119
5:19 . . . . 41, 105, 119
5:21 119
6:2 42

Galatians
2:20 23
3:2-5 127
3:28 97
4:3 41
4:4 15
5:1 41

Ephesians
1:3-6 . . . . 50–51, 59
1:7-10 46
1:10 . . . . 53, 114
1:18-23 49
2:4-7 121

2:4-8 24
2:5-8 41
2:8 . . . . 60, 138n14
2:19 54
3:8 53
3:9-10 41
3:17-19 55
3:18-21 90
6:12 121
6:17 xi

Philippians
2:6-7 43
2:6-8 13
2:10-11 95
2:12 89
2:13 89

Colossians
1 115
1:15-20 46
1:16 17
1:16-20 115
1:17 65
1:20 115

1 Thessalonians
1:2-3 42
1:4-9 126
1:5 42
3:6-9 42

1 Timothy
2:1-6 76
2:4 . . . . 45, 87

2 Timothy
2:13 . . . . 21, 49

Titus
2:11 40

Hebrews
2:16 121
10:20 100
11:1 89

12:1-3 42
12:18-19, 22 136
12:18-29 136

1 Peter
1:20 61
2:9 51
3:15 x
3:19-20 63
3:21 47
4:6 63

2 Peter
3:9 120

1 John
1:1 5
2:1-2 74
2:28 76
3:2 84

3:14 . . . . 8, 12
3:16 13
3:21 76
4:19 82

Revelation
5 45
5:11-13 44
7:9-10 89
7:10 . . . . 9, 121
19:1 9
19:19 86
21:2, 9 22
21:4 88
21:7 18
21:10-14 124
21:27 86
22:1-5 19
22:2 6
22:15 86

INDEX OF NAMES

Aaron, 16
Abel, 117
Abraham, 16, 72, 97, 112, 114, 116, 121, 123, 129
Adam, 2, 25, 74, 76–77, 114
Agrippa (king), 41
Amos, 8, 128
Anselm of Canterbury, 112–13
Attila the Hun, 18
Auden, W. H., 2
Augustine, 25, 71, 74, 75, 109, 137n8, 139n6, 140n6

Balthasar, Hans Urs von, 135
Barth, Karl
    on amateurs in faith, 28
    on Billy Graham, 127
    on creation and redemption, 47–48
    on desire that all be saved, 51
    on difference between Christian and non-Christian, 95
    on eternal damnation or reward, 75
    on formation of first church, 65
    on God's grace, 13, 50
    on gospel, 9
    on Judas, 125
    on judgment by the Resurrection, 78–79
    on justification by faith, 49
    on mercy for all, 38-39, 77
    on mercy versus judgment of God, 31
    objective" view of salvation, 49–50
    on Pontius Pilate in Apostles' Creed, 8
    on reconciliation, 29, 135
    on salvation, 4, 25, 48–49, 61–62, 76, 111, 131
    on Satan's realm, 48
    on who is saved, 119

Beckett, Samuel, 84
Bethge, Eberhard, 22
bin Laden, Osama, 18, 56
Bonhoeffer, Dietrich, 22, 73
Borg, Marcus, 103–4
Brueggemann, Walter, 122
Brunner, Emil, 80
Buber, Martin, 107
Bush, Barbara, 89
Bush, George W., 24, 71, 89, 133

Cain, 117
Calvin, John, 14, 27, 35, 50–51, 58–59, 71, 106
Catherine of Siena, 87-88
Clinton, Bill, 70
Cone, James, 114
Connor, Bull, 129
Cornelius (Centurion), 97
Cyprian, 140n6

Dante, 70
Darby, John, 59
Dawkins, Richard, 39–40
Depp, Alfred, 73
Dickinson, Emily, 133
Dodd, C. H., 137n8
Duns Scotus, John, 8
Dylan, Bob, ix

Edwards, Jonathan, 14
Elijah, 81
Elisha, 5, 81
Eve, 2

Finney, Charles, 60
Forsyth, P. T., 86
Franklin, Benjamin, 104
Freud, Sigmund, 14, 35, 37

Gabriel, 63
Gandhi, Mahatma, 18
Garbo, Greta, 74
Gibbon, Edward, 116
Gibson, Mel, 111, 113, 114
God
    authority over hell, 63, 83

baptism as act of, 30–31, 48
depiction within the parable of the fig tree, 80, 85–86
depiction within the parable of the good Samaritan, 10–11
depiction within the parable of the laborers in the vineyard, 35, 52
depiction within the parable of the lost boy, 7
depiction within the parable of the lost sheep, 40, 70–71, 84
depiction within the parable of the prodigal son, 36–37, 66–67
depiction within the parable of the talents, 82–83
disobedience to, 39
Gentiles as well as Jews serving, 38, 42, 72, 96–97, 98, 114, 118
grace of, 13, 28, 47, 50, 51, 60–62, 66, 83, 89, 95
humanity's atonement with, 17, 51, 58, 77, 112–16
identity of, 35
invitation of, to poor and dispossessed, 53–54
Islamic rending of, 23
judgment of, 3, 31, 70–92
justification of the ways of, 43
kingdom of, 6–9, 14, 48, 70, 74, 93, 98, 114, 123, 130–32
lives without reference to, 1–3
love of, 10, 21–33, 43, 45–46, 49, 56, 63, 129
mercy of, 31, 38–39, 51, 72, 79, 80
personal communication with, 14–16, 24, 62–63
reconciliation to, 27, 28, 29, 58, 69, 88, 119, 121, 135
rejection of, 50, 55, 61, 69–70, 79, 83
salvation as work of, 4-9, 24, 25, 40
salvation primarily about, 1–4
transcendence of, 16–17
union of, with humanity, 22–23, 64
and work of creation, 2–3, 4, 14–19
Graham, Billy, 60, 89, 127
Green, Joel B., 138n2
Gregory of Nyssa, 47

Hart, Frederick, 2
Hauerwas, Stanley, ix, 129
Havel, Václav, 4
Hick, John, 105
Hine, Stuart K., 113
Hitchens, Christopher, 57–58
Hitler, Adolph, 18, 45, 110, 120
Homer, 37
Hosea, 5

Irenaeus, 114
Isaiah (prophet), 5–6

Jefferson, Thomas, 104

Jeremiah (prophet), 16
Jeremy (baptized child), 29–30
Jerry (funeral of), 91
Jesus Christ
    the Advocate, 74, 75
    Beatitudes of, 6–7
    birth of, x, 7, 15
    church as bride of, 22, 119, 120
    command of, to pray for enemies, 37–38, 56
    crucifixion of, 7, 9, 21, 23, 33, 41, 55, 72, 75, 86, 98, 125
    death of, for ungodly, 17–18, 119, 135
    drawing all to himself, 64, 65, 102
    dying and rising with, 31
    enthroned, 2, 3
    of eternal life, 26–27, 42–43
    as God's definition of salvation, 10, 110
    as God with us, 5, 7–8, 11, 13, 22, 23, 75
    gospel of, ix, 89
    on handling injustices in church, 72
    and healing of nations, 6
    height of, 109–10, 112
    on hell, 72
    historical, 6, 7, 43
    the Judge, 21, 70–92
    love for, 1
    love of, 11–12, 31–33, 47, 83
    name of, 5, 64, 93–95, 97
    presence of, in Eucharist, 29, 61, 64, 93
    as prophet, 23, 75, 81
    resurrected, 5, 26–27, 64, 78–79, 95, 116
    salvation through, 6, 7, 11, 15, 50–51, 74, 97
    as Truth, 13, 94–95, 99, 100, 101, 106
    as victor, 48–49, 119
    the Way, 13, 98–107
    welcoming of sinners, 7, 40, 63, 110
    word *salvation* used in relation to, ix–xi
    as "Yes!" of God, 28, 35, 59
Job (patriarch), 16, 62
John (apostle), 108
John Paul II (pope), 45, 53
John the Baptist, 6
Joshua, 5
Judas Iscariot, 45, 125

Kant, Immanuel, 74, 117
Kennedy, James, 77–78

Kennedy, X. J., 26
Kierkegaard, Søren, 135–36
King, Martin Luther, Jr., 18

Larkin, Phillip, 86
Lazarus, 72, 73, 75
Lewis, C. S., 26, 28, 69, 84, 102
Lindsey, Hal, 43
Luke (apostle), 131
Luther, Martin, 15, 31, 45, 50, 58, 71

Maranda (student), 108
Mary (mother of Jesus), 2, 7, 23
Matthew (apostle), 5, 6–7
Moody, Dwight, 60
Moses, 4, 8, 16, 27
Muhammad, 23, 102, 107, 132, 141n12

Neuhaus, Richard, 45, 74–75, 83, 88, 90, 94, 135, 138n5
Nicodemus, 78
Niebuhr, H. Richard, 74
Nietzsche, Friedrich, 116

O'Connor, Flannery, 3, 135
Origen, 71, 72, 75, 139n6

Paul (apostle)
       on alibis offered for church decline, 131
       on church as minister of reconciliation, 119
       on Christ's death for ungodly, 17, 119
       on confessing Jesus is Lord, 124–25
       on Damascus road, 32, 97, 118
       on "dead" in sin, 120–21
       on death, 26
       on free gift of salvation, 25
       on future redemption, 88
       on God being "all in all," 87
       on God of Gentiles as well as Jews, 96–97
       on governing authorities, 83
       on Lord's judgment, 76
       on mind of the Lord, 108
       on new Adam, 114
       on personal trust of, in Jesus Christ, 32
       on plurality of salvations, x
       on power of God, 119–20
       on predestination, 59

(Paul—continued)
    on prophesying deliverer, 122
    on receptivity of gift of grace, 61
    on salvation for all, 41–43, 46, 53, 58
    on sweeping, decisive salvation of God, 115
    on triumph of Jesus, 56
    on withstanding wiles of devil, xi
    on "working out" salvation, 89
Peter (apostle)
    boldness of, 41
    denial of Jesus, 52
    Jesus telling "follow me," 98, 102
    on salvation, 9, 93–94
    on universal restoration, 47
    witnessed from jail cell, 132
Pharaoh, 4, 120
Plato, 14, 25, 26, 98
Pontius Pilate, 7, 8, 15–16, 78
Potter, Harry, 24
Pseudo-Dionysius, 64–65, 138n5

Reagan, Ronald, 70
Rodin, Auguste, 2
Rosenzweig, Franz, 55
Russert, Tim, 140n8

Satan, 43, 48, 71, 119
Saul. *See* Paul (apostle)
Silvanus, 59
Simpson, O. J., 93

Teresa, Mother, 18, 135
Thatcher, Margaret, 70
Thomas (apostle), 100, 101
Thomas (student), 108
Tillich, Paul, 15
Timothy (apostle), 59

Washington, George, 104
Wesley, Charles, 5, 33, 55–56, 139n8, 138–39n15
Wesley, John
    on alibis offered for church decline, 131
    on divine-human synergy in salvation, 16
    and fruit of prospective preachers, 132
    on God's universal love, 63
    and God's work in prisons, 132

height of, 109
  on justification link with sanctification, 118–19
  on receptivity of gift of grace, 61
  on salvation in divine life, 44
  on tense of verb *sesomenoi*, 138n14
  on triumph of grace of God, 50
  as tympanum occupant, 3
  on universal atonement versus universal salvation, 51, 58
  on "working out" salvation, 89
Willis, David, 57
Wright, N. T., 111, 114, 140n10

Zacchaeus, 109–11, 112, 114, 115, 116, 121, 122, 124, 129, 131
Zechariah, 6